BURPEE AMERICAN GARDENING SERIES
BULBS

BURPEE

AMERICAN GARDENING SERIES

BULBS

Suzanne Frutig Bales

PRENTICE HALL GARDENING
New York ◆ London ◆ Toronto ◆ Sydney ◆ Tokyo ◆ Singapore

This book is dedicated to my father, Edward C. Frutig, whose help
and encouragement made it possible.

PRENTICE HALL GENERAL REFERENCE
15 Columbus Circle
New York, NY 10023

Copyright © 1992 by Suzanne Frutig Bales

PRENTICE HALL and colophon are registered trademarks
of Simon & Schuster Inc.

BURPEE is a registered trademark of W. Atlee Burpee & Company.

Library of Congress Cataloging-in-Publication Data

Bales, Suzanne.
    The Burpee American gardening series. Bulbs / Suzanne Bales.
        p.   cm.
    Includes index.
    ISBN 0-671-86392-4
    1. Bulbs.   2. Bulbs—Pictorial works.   I. Title.   II. Title:
Bulbs.
SB425.B266   1992
635.9′44—dc20   91-15737
                                                           CIP

Designed by Patricia Fabricant and Levavi & Levavi
Manufactured in the United States of America

10   9   8   7   6   5   4

First Edition

On the cover: *Cheerful yellow tulips dazzle when they are massed together—a sea of spring color.*
Preceding pages: *In the author's garden, crown imperial stands above a field of naturalized daffodils.*
Primroses bloom at the feet of the bulbs. In the distance, Darwin hybrid tulips are beginning to open.

CONTENTS

Introduction

A new planting of bulbs is a good bet. In fact, it's as close to a "sure thing" as a gardener ever gets. Bulbs arrive complete with a potential flower or two inside, well-fed, round, firmly packed and nearly foolproof. Regardless of the skill of the gardener, bulbs bloom the first year. Failure is possible only if bulbs rot from being planted in swampy soil or if they are dug up and eaten by an animal. Bulbs are also inexpensive and a great investment. Imagine the price of a bouquet of flowers and consider the number of bulbs that can be purchased for the same money. The bouquet graces a room with its beauty for about a week. Bulbs bloom in the garden for two weeks or longer, then return faithfully year after year. When planted with care, they multiply in number and in beauty over time for many years.

Bulbs are the most reasonable of plants, obliging and easygoing. In most cases, they can be planted and then left to care for themselves. Some are so adaptable they forsake their warm origins and bravely burst into bloom even in the unfamiliar cold of northern winters.

Spring bulbs, while rarely finicky, can nevertheless be rash, impatient and impulsive. This is one of the best reasons for loving them. The most eager, snowdrops are the first to bloom; just when it seems tedious winter will never end, they appear. Even if the weather is not obliging, they bloom right through the cold, powdery dusting of snow. If caught by a blinding snow storm while in bloom, they close their eyes, folding their petals into a tight bud, and wait patiently for the sun. Less than showy, snowdrops are the Houdinis of flowers, their feats are so impressive. They cheerfully take their beatings from the damaging freezing and thawing of winter, rarely showing scars, and their welcome appearance restores calm and peace to the gardener and brings assurance that spring is finally on its way.

On the first balmy winter day, notice the appearance of green shoots that dart upward through thawing ground. This emergence is extraordinary, well deserving our admiration. Spring-blooming bulbs of all kinds are not discouraged by snow and ice, but wait patiently for their next opportunity to push up another few inches. The cold earth is hard for a shovel to penetrate, yet snowdrops manage to grow. With enough warmth and sunshine they open, but like true skeptics they are always prepared for foul weather. If you wander through the garden on an early spring evening you will notice how *Anemone* closes and bends over at night, presenting the duller tints of its outer surfaces. A few weeks earlier, on an overcast day, you might have noticed the crocus and winter aconite closed up tight. Only on sunny days will the drooping flowers of *Anemone* stand up and open wide, and only then will the tightly closed crocus and winter aconite open their golden cups. These flowers usually keep normal business hours, opening at eight or nine o'clock in the morning and closing at five or six o'clock each evening. However, if the day is cloudy, rainy or snowy, the blooms remain closed, "sleeping" through the bad weather. (If these same flowers are gathered and brought into a warm room, they will soon open and remain open throughout the day and night, even if put in a dark cupboard, provided they are kept warm. The opening and closing of spring bulbs is mainly a response to changes in temperature. Essentially, their closing is a response that protects their pollen and nectar from the elements.)

Bulbs is a word loosely used by gardeners and horticulturists alike to describe the category of plants with a bulbous structure that sends anchoring roots downward and a shoot upward through the soil; the bulbs are harvested, stored, shipped and sold while in a dormant condition. The term *bulb* has come to include everything from "true bulbs" to corms, rhizomes and tubers. It is easy to confuse these because they behave similarly in the garden. Regardless of the classification, the most important

Tulips bloom at the edge of a woodland. Their dying foliage will later be hidden by the emerging hosta.

thing to remember is that they are all underground, self-contained storehouses of food for the plant. Each plant of this type is herbaceous, dying down in winter, leaving no permanent stem above ground. Thin, threadlike, feeding roots grow out from the bottom to anchor the bulb in the soil and to take in water and nutrients, but the bulbs' real energy is manufactured above ground. If an overzealous gardener, anxious to clean up a bed, removes the dying leaves too early, the bulb too will die, or the plant will offer a diminished bloom the following season (depending on how prematurely the foliage has been removed). The foliage of bulb, corm, rhizome and tuber plants must have the opportunity to yellow and die without disturbance, for this is the time when the underground storehouse is replenishing its food supply.

There are differences between bulbs, corms, tubers and rhizomes:

BULB: A bulb increases by offshoots from the mother bulb. The mother bulb will continue to live, year after year, in nutritious, well-drained soil. If you slice a bulb vertically in half, you will see the embryo leaves, stems and flower bud as well as the stored food that surrounds them. The stem starts at the bottom of the bulb and grows up through it. After blooming and while the foliage is dying back, the embryo, leaves and flower buds are produced. This accounts for the reason some bulbs, like paperwhite narcissus and hyacinth, are completely self-sufficient and will bloom even when the roots are placed in water only. The bulbs are planners-ahead that carry with them their own food supplies for their next bloom. The bulb mass is formed in layers or rings, like those of onions or

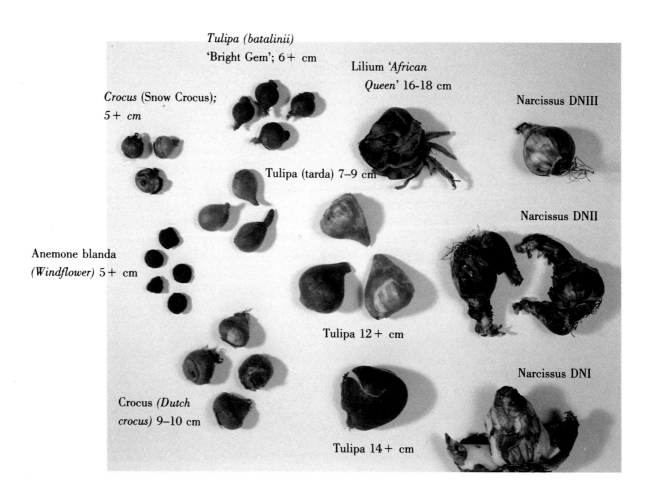

Tulipa (batalinii) 'Bright Gem'; 6+ cm

Lilium 'African Queen' 16-18 cm

Narcissus DNIII

Crocus (Snow Crocus); 5+ cm

Tulipa (tarda) 7–9 cm

Narcissus DNII

Anemone blanda *(Windflower)* 5+ cm

Tulipa 12+ cm

Narcissus DNI

Crocus *(Dutch crocus)* 9–10 cm

Tulipa 14+ cm

like the scales of an artichoke. The daffodil, lily and tulip are true bulbs.

CORM: A corm has a hard, solid body that, if cut through, will show a solid mass of food without any visible leaves or buds. A corm lives for a year, producing a new corm or corms before it dies. The immature corms are nourished by the mother corm, which gradually shrivels and dies as the immature corms deplete it. The stem grows up from the top of the corm. The crocus, gladiola and *Colchicum* grow from corms.

TUBER: A tuber, like a potato, has "eyes" or growth buds on a thickened portion of underground stem. The developing plant feeds on food stored in the tuber until its roots are developed. *Cyclamen*, winter aconite and *Oxalis* grow from tubers.

RHIZOME: A rhizome is a thick or fleshy underground stem or branch that stores food for the plant. Unlike true bulbs, these underground stems grow laterally and can send up new shoots from buds at various points along its length. Iris and Virginia bluebell (*Mertensia*) grow from rhizomes.

Throughout the book, I will use the term *bulb* to cover all four classifications when discussing their common uses. Specific information as to classification is given for each plant in the "Plant Portraits" chapter.

Because of the longevity of most bulbs, it is a common belief that bulbs are planted just once, not added to every year. Not every bulb will "return" with bloom reliably season after season, so for the most lush display more should be interplanted. I plant more every year and wonder how so many people can live without them. There are so many gorgeous bulbs from which to choose, and so little time to enjoy them because their season seems so brief. Bulbs are an inexpensive investment that returns more bulbs to the gardener each year. Even in the smallest of gardens, there is always room for more bulbs. There can never be too much of something so wonderful! Consider their dormant size, and just think: that is all the space they need! (In early fall each bulb will send out roots resembling white thread. The roots will supply the bulb with nutrients and water from the soil while the bulb is active, then die back at the same time the foliage dies back; the cycle is repeated.) Couldn't you squeeze a few more bulbs under a shrub, between crevices in a stone wall, around stepping stones, in the lawn, under groundcovers and with perennials? Always, somewhere, there is room for more.

PLANNING AND DESIGNING WITH BULBS

When it comes to planning, the sky's the limit, and that is the place to start. Too often we only look down when planning where to plant our bulbs. Start with the tops of your trees. If they are flowering, what color are the flowers, and when do they bloom? You might design a flowering bulb skirt of complementary colors, blooming through a shade-loving groundcover at the base of the tree. If it is a deciduous tree, losing its leaves each year, when does it leaf-out? Any bulb requiring full sun will bloom happily beneath it as long as it has time for its foliage to ripen before the tree is fully leafed-out. Does your tree have an interesting bark? White birch trees are very picturesque when surrounded by densely planted, deep blue grape hyacinth (a minimum planting of 250 grape hyacinth is needed to make a really good showing).

After you have contemplated how to dress up your trees, drop your sights a little lower, to the shrubs in your garden. Evergreens can be a dramatic backdrop for flowering bulbs. Colors bounce off the rich, deep green background and appear to come forward. The gray-blue of blue spruce is an unusual and colorful complement to yellow tulips, Virginia bluebells and daffodils. The shiny, deep green leaves of boxwood heighten and enhance the colors of bright tulips planted in front of them.

Flowering shrubs are the perfect backdrop for, or centerpiece in the midst of, spring bulbs.

The blue of grape hyacinth complements the white bark of the birch tree.

Wood hyacinths naturalize and increase freely under deciduous azaleas.

This woodland path is lined with the color of daffodils, Virginia bluebells and species tulips.

Make the most of their beauty and build your garden picture around them. Consider the colors of your shrubs in bloom. Many azaleas, for example, come in bright, shocking—almost neon—colors, tricky to combine with other colors. Don't plant your bulbs without coordinating their color with the flowering shrubs. Clashing colors can be hard on the eyes, not something you look forward to seeing year after year.

The following list will give you some ideas for combining flowering shrubs and trees with bulbs. These suggestions are just a start. More than one type of bulb can be planted under or around these shrubs and trees to make a fuller, more exuberant picture. Just remember that bulbs scattered around the yard instead of grouped with other flowering plants lose their impact. Of course they are beautiful, but they could be much more so if they focused our attention on a garden picture. Scattered, their effect is dissipated and their potential underused. Bear in mind too that all bulbs look better when planted under a groundcover. Bare soil, especially in early spring, distracts the eye; the brown of soil doesn't complement or enhance flower colors.

COMBINATIONS WITH FLOWERING SHRUBS OR TREES (Month of Bloom in Zone 7)

FEBRUARY

Cornus sericea, red-twig dogwood (red bark), with snowdrops* (white)

Daphne Mezereum*, February daphne (white), with glory-of-the-snow (blue)

Hamamelis mollis*, witch hazel (yellow or orange), with snowdrops* (white), glory-of-the-snow (blue) or winter aconite (yellow)

Jasminum nudiflorium*, jasmine (yellow), with glory-of-the-snow (blue)

Salix discolor, pussy willow (silver-gray), with snowdrops* (white), glory-of-the-snow (blue) or winter aconite (yellow)

MARCH

Cotoneaster horizontalis, rock cotoneaster (burgundy foliage with red berries), with dwarf iris* (yellow)

Forsythia, golden bells (yellow), surrounded by daffodils* 'February Gold' (yellow) and glory-of-the-snow (blue)

Leucothoe Fontanesiana, drooping leucothoe (burgundy foliage), with early daffodils* and glory-of-the-snow (blue)

Magnolia stellata*, star magnolia (white), with Siberian squill (blue) and miniature daffodils* (yellow and white)

Prunus Jacquemontii*, flowering-almond, with late-blooming daffodils* and Virginia bluebells (blue and pink)

APRIL

Fothergilla Gardenii*, witch alder (white), with Virginia bluebells (blue)

Mahonia*, leatherleaf mahonia (yellow), with grape hyacinth* (blue)

Pieris japonica*, Japanese andromeda (white), with species tulips

MAY

Enkianthus campanulatus (white with red), with tulips* or wood hyacinth (pink, blue or white)

Kalmia latifolia, mountain laurel (white or rose), with wood hyacinth (pink, blue or white)

*Fragrant varieties of these flowers and shrubs are available.

Malus floribunda, flowering crab apple (pink), with tulips* (pink, yellow or white)

Rhododendron, azalea (white, yellow or pink), with wood hyacinth (pink, blue or white)

Viburnum, American cranberry bush (white), with tulips* (any color)

JUNE

Rhododendron, rhododendron (white or pink), with iris

*Styrax japonicus**, Japanese snowball (white), with assorted bearded iris

*Syringa**, lilac (pink, white or lilac), with bearded iris

Weigela (red), with summer snowflakes (white)

JULY

*Clethra alnifolia**, summer sweet (white or pink), with *Lilium*, lilies* (pastel colors)

Hydrangea (blue or pink), with dahlias (pastel colors)

*Koelreuteria paniculata**, golden-rain tree (yellow), with *Lilium*, Asian lilies* (orange, yellow and red)

Potentilla fruticosa, cinquefoil (bright yellow), with *Lilium*, Asian lilies* (orange, yellow and red)

AUGUST

Buddleia Davidii, butterfly bush (purple or white), with *Lilium*, lilies (soft pastel colors)

*Vitex**, chaste tree (blue), with *Lycoris*, magre lily* (pastel colors)

SEPTEMBER

Hydrangea, oak-leafed hydrangea (white), with autumn crocus (pink)

OCTOBER

Hydrangea, any variety, with *Crocus speciosus*, fall-blooming crocus (purple)

FRAGRANCE IN THE GARDEN

Who can walk through a house with chocolate chip cookies in the oven and not head for the kitchen? Favorite Sunday dinners are the ones that stew, roast or bake for several hours as the family enjoys the aroma of dinner long before it is served. Familiar and pleasant fragrances are comforting and lift the spirits. Isn't this one of the reasons we send flowers to the sick? The fragrance of flowers in bloom cheers us. Any child can identify the smell of bubble gum, but how many have been taught to bend down and smell a snowdrop or to pause and take a deep breath when passing a clump of sweet-smelling lily of the valley? The forgotten pleasures of natural fragrance and the enjoyment it brings are worth remembering and sharing with our children.

Most gardens are planned meticulously for color and long bloom, but fragrance is usually overlooked. Garden planners often seem to be unmindful of fragrance. Perhaps, with the availability of commercial, artificial scents, we have overlooked the natural garden fragrances. We live with artificially scented tissues, powders, soaps, cleaning agents and potpourri, not to mention perfume. The difference between the natural scent of a bouquet of flowers and perfume is dramatic.

The fragrance of bulbs varies from the sweet (some smell like honey) to the tart (lemon is a common touch) and on to the heavily musky. There is an intimate quality to a fragrant garden that beckons you in, insists that you linger and, at times, pulls you down to its level to

breathe in the enchanting fragrances that surround you. Fragrance travels farthest on days that are both warm and moist; the high heat and drought of summer repress the scent of flowers. Controversy abounds as to which fragrances are pleasant and which are overwhelming or downright repugnant. The heavy, richly sweet scent of paperwhite narcissus is a good example. This pretty flower is either loved or hated. A bowl of paperwhites placed in a living room will scent every adjoining room as well. As the blooms age and fade, the scent becomes even more intense. Walking in the garden, you'll notice their scent will reach you before you see them, even if there are as few as a dozen in bloom.

In nature there are no hard

Lilies of the valley bloom through a groundcover of ajuga and in front of a Jack-in-the-pulpit.

and fast rules, but a few generalizations can be made. The majority of fragrant flowers are white; bright, boldly colored flowers are seldom scented. The sweetest-smelling flowers are sometimes not much to look at. It's as though a lovely fragrance were consolation for a less-than-spectacular appearance. The lightly colored flowers such as the purples, pinks and mauves are frequently scented. Thick-petaled, waxy flowers are also often heavily scented, for example, the rose, the gardenia, the lily and the tuberose.

Fragrance is sometimes found in the foliage rather than the flower. In the case of some bulbs it is as though the scent were tightly guarded, released only when the foliage is touched. Other flowers, such as lilies, spontaneously release their fragrance to drift on the wind, wafting into the house through open windows and inviting us out. A timid few, like moonflower, hide their fragrance until dusk and then grace the evening with their perfume. Some, like the vanilla-fragrant snowflake (*Leucojum*), need the warmth of a hand or a heated room to release their fragrance. Still others send mixed fragrances; the spring starflower's (*Ipheion*) flowers smell like mint and its leaves, if bruised or crushed, release an onion fragrance.

Many of the tiny spring bulbs (among them snowdrops, crocus and blue puschkinia) are fragrant, but because of their small size and because they usually are planted in small groups, it's hard for them to make their presence known. They deserve a stage where they can be admired while they scent the air. Planted on top of a stone wall they may be more accessible—they can be admired without stooping.

When flowers are hybridized for dwarfness, longer bloom and disease resistance, the first characteristic the flower loses is its fragrance. Scent alone is reason enough to look again at the old-fashioned varieties, their fragrance unspoiled by hybridizing. It's to be hoped that breeders will soon learn nature's secret of fragrance and be able to keep it even as they improve flowers' growing qualities.

The wonderful spring starflowers have a sweet mint fragrance, but if the leaves are bruised they smell mildly of onions.

Be sure to place a container planting of your favorite fragrant bulbs (here, a lushly planted tub of hyacinths) where you can enjoy their lovely scent.

FRAGRANT BULBS

Amaryllis (belladonna lily)
Convallaria (lily of the valley)
Crocus biflorus (crocus)
Crocus Imperati (crocus)
Erythronium Dens-canis (dogtooth violet)
Galanthus (snowdrops)
Hyacinthus (hyacinth)
Leucojum vernum (snowflakes)
Lilium (lily)
Muscari conicum 'Heavenly Blue' (grape hyacinth)
Muscari moschatum (grape hyacinth)
Narcissus (daffodil)
Puschkinia (blue puschkinia)
Scilla nutans (squill)
Tulipa (tulip)

COLOR

Gardening effectively with color is a fine art. Careful consideration of color arrangement is important, because harmonious color schemes happen by accident only infrequently. You can never overestimate the simple magic of color for its own sake. The audacity of nature is displayed in the extraordinary colors of bulbs. There are colors that dazzle, colors that shock, quiet colors that make an impression only viewed close-up and colors that alone are seemingly washed out, but have the unselfish ability to enhance a neighbor.

Tulips epitomize the glorious range of flower colors available today. There are tulips in every tint from velvety violet to delicate buff, soft salmon, vivid orange and neon pink to the almost black. The only shades missing from the tulip spectrum are a true blue and a true black. (Breeders have been working to bring black, the one color nature passed over entirely, to the garden. So far a deep purple tulip, sometimes called "black," is available. I personally side with nature and don't see a reason for black, although I tried "black" tulips once and found them arresting in the garden.)

Flower color changes depending on what is next to it, so discretion and planning are important. A color can be enhanced or overshadowed. A bright, gaudy color next to a soft color often makes it appear washed out, pale and anemic. Warring colors distract from the garden's beauty. If strong colors are your taste, nature has provided a palette to take your breath away. I caution you to limit each area of the garden to three colors the first year. Pick colors that you would wear together or combine in decorating a room in your house. Gardens should not be a mishmash of unconnected color, nor should they require less attention than you spend on your wardrobe. Plan meticulously for color and group variously colored flowers with care. Sometimes it's helpful if you consider natural color groups for sure-fire combinations. Red, yellow and orange are the colors of the sunset, and blue, purple and white are the colors of a rolling ocean on a sunny day. Purple, orange and yellow are the flaming colors of fire.

In early spring strong colors are absent from the garden. Yellows, whites and blues dominate the early bulbs. At that time of year, it is impossible to combine colors that don't complement each other. The discrete use of the stronger colors that begin to appear at the end of spring can brighten an area otherwise dull because summer flowers are just coming up and there is the eyesore of bare soil. Strangely enough, the bold colors (yellow, orange and scarlet) show up best in bright sunshine whereas the gentle colors (white, lavender, violet and blue) are best in shade where they become distinct. Sunlight overpowers the meek; gentle colors fade, dim and wash out in bright daylight. If colors did not combine as you had hoped, it is easy enough to move them, by taking the bulbs up as soon as they finish blooming.

The ivory-white petals of 'Shirley' tulips, delicately edged with light purple, are complemented by the deep purple of pansies.

Far left: *Bulbs are an invaluable addition to the gardener's palette, adding brilliant accents to the glorious profusion of seasonal color.*

Left: *Red tulips appear brighter when offset by yellow tulips striped with red.*

WINNING COMBINATIONS OF BULBS

Tulips blooming through a sea of blue forget-me-nots (Myosotis).

Virginia bluebells blooming with white tulips.

Violet-colored pansies surrounding pink and yellow tulips.

Two early bloomers are snowdrops and winter aconite.

Lilium canadense blooms in a white mist of Thalictrum.

Miniature daffodil 'Tête-à-Tête' is naturalized with glory-of-the-snow.

The late-winter blooming daffodil 'February Gold' is a good companion for the winter-blooming Helleborus ×hybridus orientalis.

Tulip 'Yellow King' complements grape hyacinth.

Burpee's Lemon Chiffon collection features Narcissus 'Hawera', forget-me-nots and Muscari botryoides 'Album'.

NATURALIZING BULBS

Naturalizing means to imitate nature. Large groups of bulbs are naturalized when planted together in free-form groups, not lined up like soldiers in a parade. The usual way to do this is to plant an imitation of a stream that widens here, narrows there, as it lazily meanders between trees and around shrubs. One traditional method of deciding where to plant each bulb is to take a handful and scatter them across the prepared soil; the bulbs then are planted where they have fallen. Another method is to plant in irregular drifts, allowing one sweep to taper off as it leads to another.

Some bulbs may be naturalized in grass, interplanted with a groundcover (such as pachysandra or vinca) or in a woods. The early, tiny spring bulbs that bloom and die back before the lawn needs mowing are the easiest bulbs to grow in a lawn. The grass protects them from spatterings of mud kicked up by spring rains while it enhances their color with a carpet of green. Small bulbs are not planted deeply and a corner of sod needs only to be turned back to allow a half dozen bulbs to be tucked underneath without leaving a trace. Larger bulbs, such as daffodils and wood hyacinths, can also be planted in the lawn; in this case a section of sod—as deep as the grass roots reach—needs to be removed, a hole dug, the bulbs planted and the sod replaced. The disadvantage of larger and later-blooming bulbs is that the grass cannot be mowed until late June when the bulb foliage has yellowed.

Unless you want a wild meadow, this can make for an unsightly patch of lawn.

The bulbs used in naturalizing must be chosen carefully to ensure they can take care of themselves with little help from the gardener, increasing yearly if initially planted in well-prepared soil. Spring bulbs are particularly effective when used this way. Crocus and daffodils are probably the bulbs that first come to mind when one thinks of naturalizing, but there is a host of spring-blooming bulbs that deserve to be better known and lend themselves particularly well to naturalized plantings. When naturalizing, it is usually impractical to dig up the entire area. Bulbs may be planted individually or in clumps, planting several bulbs of one variety in a larger hole or trench. I like trenches that vary in width, swelling and receding. In trenches, the bulbs are planted all at once instead of one at a time, and the clusters look more natural.

Mulching is not necessary for naturalized bulbs where grass, groundcover or fallen leaves provide a natural cover. But after planting the bulbs be sure to water them well.

All the bulbs in the list of recommendations for naturalizing that follows are suitable for interplanting with each other. Just mix and match them however you desire. The greater the number of varieties of bulbs planted, the longer the period of bloom can be extended. Interplant them to achieve an early, midseason and late

Snowdrops, the earliest bulbs to bloom, have been naturalized at Winterthur gardens.

Winter aconite welcomes spring with bright, buttercup-yellow bloom. An excellent choice for naturalizing, the low-growing, sometimes long-blooming plants feature handsome foliage.

period of bloom or use them to complement and enlarge existing plantings. Refer to "Plant Portraits" to see whether they are tolerant of either sun or shade and can be planted in a meadow or woodland. All are long lived and will provide enjoyment and beauty for generations.

Naturalized daffodils and snowflakes bloom in the glow of a forsythia bush.

Chionodoxa (glory-of-the-snow) and *Galanthus* (snowdrops)
Eranthis (winter aconite) and *Galanthus* (snowdrops)
Eranthis (winter aconite) and *Chionodoxa* (glory-of-the-snow)
Leucojum vernum (spring snowflakes) and *Chionodoxa* (glory-of-the-snow)
Narcissus (early daffodil) and *Puschkinia* (blue puschkinia)
Narcissus (late daffodil) and *Mertensia* (Virginia bluebell)
Narcissus (daffodil) and *Scilla siberica* (Siberian squill)
Miniature *Narcissus* ('Hawera') and *Muscari botryoides* ('Album')
Miniature *Narcissus* and *Crocus* (spring crocus)

BULBS FOR NATURALIZING

Allium caeruleum (flowering onion)
Anemone blanda (Greek windflower)
Camassia Leichtlinii (camass)
Chionodoxa Luciliae (glory-of-the-snow)
Colchicum (autumn crocus)
Crocus (spring crocus)
Endymion hispanicus (wood hyacinth)
Eranthis hyemalis (winter aconite)
Galanthus nivalis (snowdrops)
Iris bucharica (dwarf iris)
Iris Danfordiae (dwarf iris)
Iris reticulata (dwarf iris)
Leucojum aestivum (snowflakes)
Mertensia virginica (Virginia bluebell)
Muscari armeniacum (grape hyacinth)
Narcissus (daffodil)
Puschkinia (blue puschkinia)

CARPETS FOR BULBS

Let groundcovers be the workhorses of the garden. They will protect the bulbs from freezing and thawing weather, keep mud from splattering them, provide them with a backdrop and stage for their performance, enhance their colors and gracefully hide their unsightly exits. A groundcover can even lend a helping hand to floppy flowers that lack backbone, supporting them so they stand up after heavy beatings from rain, wind and snow. As the bulbs fade, the ground below stays green. Smaller bulbs should be planted in low-growing groundcovers so they don't drown in the greens. Bulbs, like people, want good neighbors and carefully selected groundcovers make perfect neighbors for them.

GROUNDCOVERS FOR UNDERPLANTING BULBS

Blue grape hyacinth bloom in the midst of foam flowers (Tiarella).

Ajuga (bugleweed)
Aubrieta (rainbow rock cress)
Cerastium (snow-in-summer)
Chrysogonum virginianum (goldenstar)
Cornus canadensis (bunchberry)
Dicentra eximia (fringed bleeding heart)
Epimedium (barrenwort)
Euonymus Fortunei 'Colorata' (purple-leaf wintercreeper)
Euonymus Fortunei 'Gracilis' (creeping variegated euonymus)
Euonymus Fortunei 'Minima' (euonymus)
Galium odoratum (sweet woodruff)
Hedera Helix (Boston ivy)
Hosta (funkia)
Iberis sempervirens (candytuft)
Liriope (lilyturf)
Lysimachia Nummularia (creeping Jennie)
Mazus reptans (mazus)
Nepeta × Faassenii (catmint)
Pachysandra (spurge)
Phlox divaricata (woodland phlox)
Phlox subulata (creeping phlox)
Pulmonaria (lungwort)
Sedum (stonecrop)
Stachys (lamb's ears)
Thymus (thyme)
Tiarella (foamflower)
Veronica repans (creeping speedwell)
Vinca minor (periwinkle)

BULBS IN DESIGN

The gaiety of spring bulbs turns a garden into a frolicking playground, lively with the coming and going of little flowers. One group drifts in and mingles while another departs. Most spring bulbs stay in bloom for a few weeks, with good weather perhaps three or more, but by including groups of different varieties the spring parade can be long and dazzling. Don't be tempted to mix different bulbs and plant them haphazardly. Jack-in-the-box planting of bulbs, one popping up here, another popping up over there, is an all-too-common error. Plant a dozen or more of one sort next to two dozen of another, and weave a third and fourth variety around, behind or out in front of the first two. Remember that bulbs planted in straight lines resemble nothing so much as a parade of pastel penguins marching through the garden, and that is not the best presentation.

Avoid "special price" collections that include one or two bulbs of many varieties. Mixed clutter is not attractive. Collections large enough to include a dozen or more of one bulb color coordinated with another bulb will be more attractive. Simple groupings of single varieties are foolproof, always pleasing.

Clustered and massed bulbs show off their beauty even from a distance. Disarray is charming in a naturalized planting where one group of bulbs gracefully spills over into another. The challenge of bulbs, as you've probably guessed, is not in the growing. Even friends of mine who don't consider themselves gardeners grow them successfully, with minimum effort. The challenge is combining bulbs of different varieties with groundcovers, perennials, annuals, shrubs and trees. Just as people are improved by the company they keep, plants shine when surrounded by friends.

Bulbs are gregarious creatures. They love a party. The larger the party, the better dressed and better behaved they become. They help each other deal with changeable spring weather. It is a common misconception that each plant needs its own square footage. The bulbs themselves are indifferent to how closely they are planted, except when they are almost touching. These delightful flowers find protection in numbers against lashing wind, pelting snow, pounding hail and drowning rain. And as if these trials weren't enough, bulbs frequently suffer the humiliation of mud-spattered new clothes. As gardeners it is up to us to be sensitive to their plight and help them when and where we can. It is a simple matter to protect spring-blooming bulbs by carefully massing them or putting them under the protective care of an evergreen or early appearing groundcover.

Think of bulbs as city dwellers living in underground apartments. The smallest bulbs prefer the penthouses just below the surface. The larger the bulbs, the deeper they should be planted, with the largest bulbs settling into the basement rooms. Instinctively, their stems know how to grow up and around each other, requiring only a small space for their roots and body in a nutritious and well-drained soil. A rule of thumb is to plant each bulb to a depth of three times the largest diameter of the bulb (*Colchicum* is the one exception, preferring shallow planting). The inches recommended in the "Plant Portraits" chapter bulb guides and on bulb packaging for the depth of planting of a bulb refer to the distance from the top of the bulb to ground level.

Naturalized daffodils with yellow crown imperial.

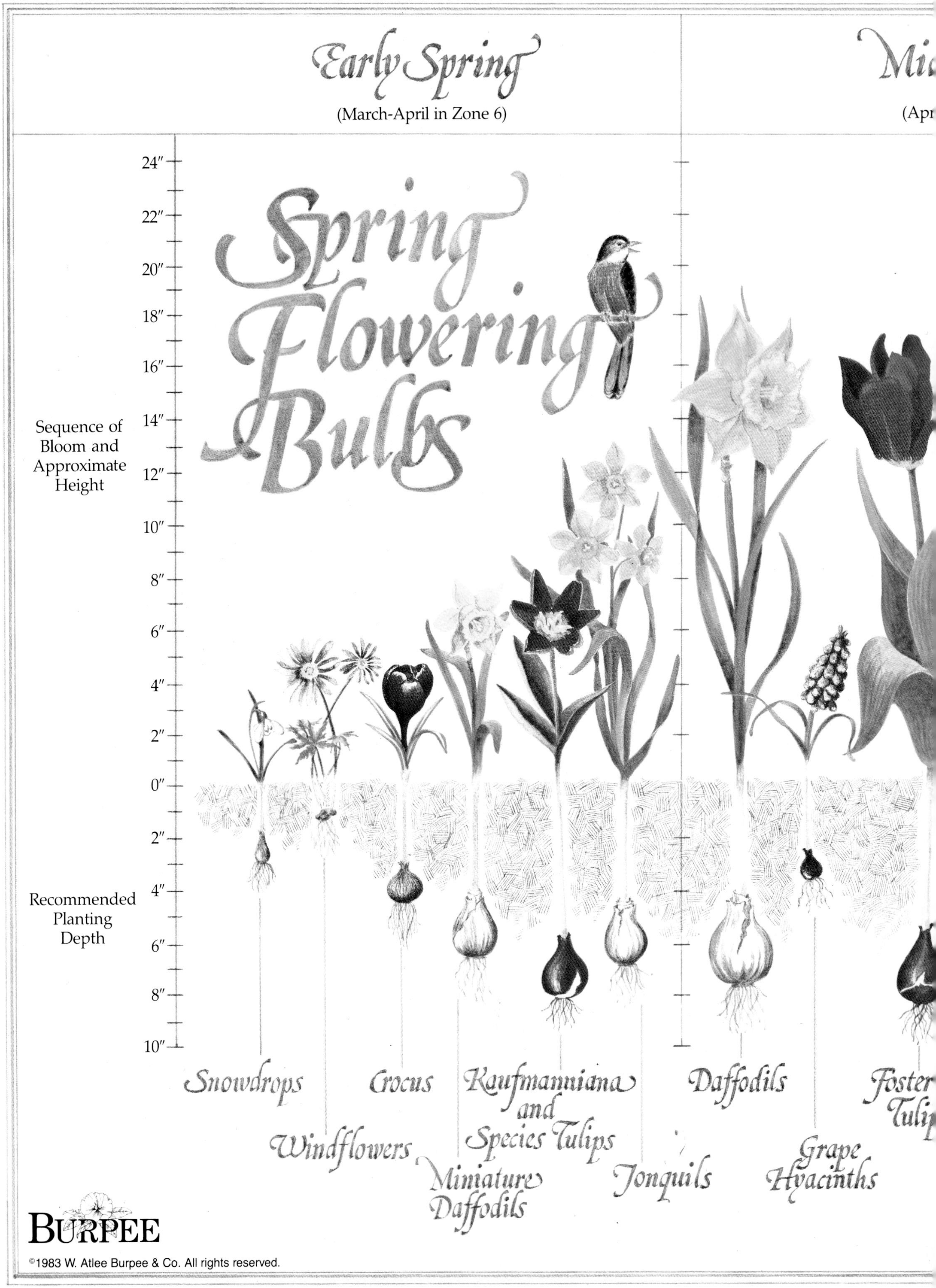
Early Spring
(March-April in Zone 6)
Mid
(Apr
Spring Flowering Bulbs
Sequence of Bloom and Approximate Height
24″
22″
20″
18″
16″
14″
12″
10″
8″
6″
4″
2″
0″
2″
4″
6″
8″
10″
Recommended Planting Depth
Snowdrops
Windflowers
Crocus
Miniature Daffodils
Kaufmanniana and Species Tulips
Jonquils
Daffodils
Grape Hyacinths
Foster
Tuli
BURPEE

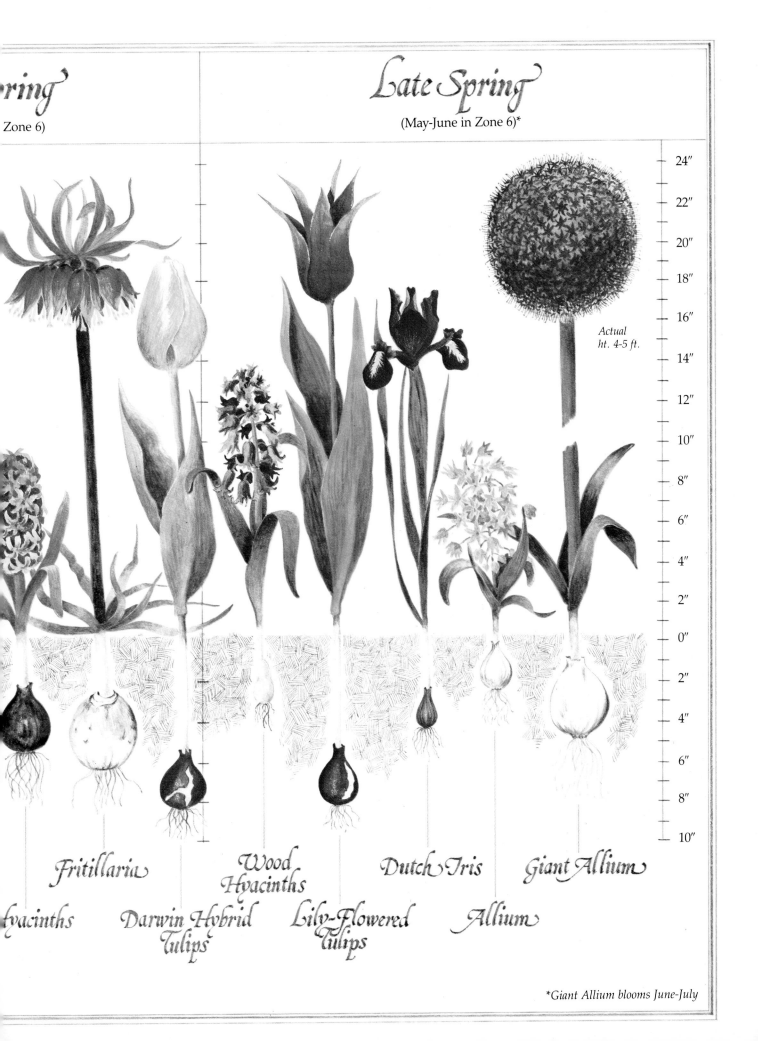

24″
22″
20″
18″
16″
14″
12″
10″
8″
6″
4″
2″
0″
2″
4″
6″
8″
10″

Actual ht. 4-5 ft.

Fritillaria

Wood Hyacinths

Dutch Iris

Giant Allium

Hyacinths

Darwin Hybrid Tulips

Lily-Flowered Tulips

Allium

*Giant Allium blooms June-July

As the naturalized daffodils finish flowering, the hosta leaves will grow and hide their dying foliage.

Designing with Spring Bulbs

Visualize a mixed planting of large and small bulbs. Imagine preparing a hole 10 inches deep, about the width and circumference of a dinner plate. In the bottom of the hole, place 2 inches of well-drained, compost-enriched soil (see pages 30–31). Place one crown imperial (*Fritillaria imperialis*) in the center of this, and surround with six 'Cheerfulness' daffodils, equally spaced on top of the soil. Cover with more soil until the hole is 4 inches from the surface. Place three tubers of Virginia bluebell (*Mertensia virginica*) nearby, and equidistant from, the outside of the hole. Then completely cover the bluebells with 1 inch of soil. The final layer consists of small snowdrop bulbs, 12 to 18, equally spaced in the shallow hole. Cover them with soil and water well to give their roots a good drink. The snowdrops will bloom a month or two earlier than the other bulbs, returning to sleep before the Virginia bluebells and daffodils awake. The *Fritillaria*, daffodils and the Virginia bluebells will bloom together, growing to the same height; the shape and color of the Virginia bluebells will complement the yellow trumpets of the daffodils.

If you want to take this planting a step farther, plan to dig your hole between three hosta or *Astilbe* plants. These break dormancy as the bulbs finish and grow up to cover the bulbs' dying foliage. (They'll remain all summer and into fall. The colorful plumes of *Astilbe*—white, pink or red—bloom in early to midsummer and will dry right on the plant and remain interesting in the garden for months.) This grouping of bulbs and perennials could be repeated, planted in drifts instead of circles, around the trunk of a spring-flowering tree or in front of a spring-flowering shrub.

How close together you plant bulbs is a matter of taste. Do you prefer to see the outline of an individual flower and its foliage, or do you like overlap? In either case I recommend bulbs be planted closer than is recommended in the planting guides furnished by professional bulb growers. They recommend planting far apart to allow the bulbs room to multiply over the years without crowding, and this usually means that 8 inches or a foot of brown soil shows between the flowers, distracting from their beauty and frequently becoming cluttered with remnants of fall leaves. Daffodils planted far apart won't require division for 8 or 10 years, but the first 3 years will be sparse, emphasizing the naked ground.

Must you wait several years for a full, lush look? There are ways around it. Plant the bulbs under an evergreen groundcover such as *Pachysandra* or *Vinca minor*. The bulbs will be protected during the mud season and, wreathed in green, they'll appear lush and full. Create an Oriental carpet effect, with the green groundcover as background: Weave a design of bright blooms in a groundcover underplanting. Repeat groups of a dozen or more bulbs of the same variety and color, alternating them with two or more groups of other complementary bulbs that bloom at the same time. For the most natural effect, each grouping should be randomly placed.

Designing with Summer Bulbs

Most summer-blooming bulbs, such as gladiolas and dahlias (*Bletilla*, lilies and *Lycoris squamigera* are notable exceptions), are native to the warmer growing areas of the world. As such, they are not reliably winter hardy in northern areas and need to be dug up in fall and stored over winter in a frost-free area. They are planted in the garden after all danger of frost is past and must be planted where you can dig without disturbing other plants. This may sound like a lot of trouble, but they do contribute a great deal of summer color to the garden, staying in bloom for several months. Many of the summer bulbs are outstanding for cutting; if you don't relish the idea of "robbing" your flower garden

Spring-flowering Hardy Bulbs for Southern Gardens (Zones 8 to 10)

To produce flowers, most spring-flowering bulbs need an extended dormant period with cold temperatures during winter. For southern gardens, there are two classes of spring-flowering bulbs to consider. There are bulbs that can be planted in fall without any special preplanting treatment, and some of these return while some do not. Then there are bulbs that must be given preplanting, cold-storage treatment in order for them to perform satisfactorily. The latter bulbs require cooling, refrigerated in their shipping bags at 40° to 45°F, prior to planting. These bulbs have varying requirements as to the length of the cool-storage period. Tulips need 14 to 15 weeks; hyacinths, 10 to 12; crocus, 4; snowdrops and scillas, 6 to 7 and grape hyacinths, 12 to 13 weeks before they can be planted outdoors in late November and December.

A word of caution: When precooling the bulbs in the refrigerator, do not store any fruit in the same refrigerator. Ripening fruit gives off ethylene gas, which inhibits flowering.

One very important caveat for gardeners in the Deep South to consider when planting spring-flowering bulbs: Bulbs should be planted in an area that does not receive direct sunlight from late morning to late afternoon. This helps moderate the temperatures and keep the flowers in bloom longer. For the same reason, southern exposures are not very desirable. Be certain that the garden soil is well drained and the pH is between 6 and 7.

The bulbs listed usually don't need precooling in Zone 8 (they will in Zones 9 and 10). They should be planted in the garden in late November or December for spring bloom.

Allium aflatunense (flowering onion)

Allium Christophii (star of Persia)

Allium karataviense (Turkish onion)

Allium Moly (yellow allium)

Allium neapolitanum (flowering onion)

Allium sphaerocephalum (drumstick allium)

Anemone blanda (windflower)

Crocus (crocus)

Endymion hispanicus (wood hyacinth)

Hyacinthus (hyacinth)

Iris reticulata (dwarf iris)

Iris Danfordiae (dwarf iris)

Muscari armeniacum (grape hyacinth)

Narcissus (daffodil), single types

Oxalis adenophylla (wood sorrel)

Puschkinia libanotica (blue puschkinia)

Scilla siberica (Siberian squill)

Tulipa (tulip), tall cultivars only

Deep South gardens (Zones 9 and 10): Bulbs listed below don't need precooling prior to planting, but they should be considered as annual bulbs—they do not return and won't naturalize readily in the Deep South.

Allium neapolitanum (flowering onion)

Crocus chrysanthus (snow crocus)

Endymion hispanicus (wood hyacinth)

Iris (Dutch iris)

Narcissus cyclamineus, N. Jonquilla and N. triandrus 'Thalia' (daffodil)

Narcissus 'Ziva' (paperwhite narcissus)

Ornithogalum umbellatum (star-of-bethlehem)

Note: Some areas of Zone 8 don't receive 10 to 12 weeks of winter weather (below 50°F). If you live in such an area, handle the bulbs as described for the Deep South gardens.

The bare bottoms of the lilies are hidden by the foliage and red plumes of astilbe.

The soft blooms of Colchicum *'Waterlily' are unharmed by the prickly foliage of creeping phlox* (Phlox subulata).

A dwarf canna lily blooms in a pot on a terrace.

plantings, plant some summer bulbs in a vegetable or cutting garden to bring in for bouquets for the house. Some of the summer bulbs are very inexpensive—less than an annual seedling—and can be repeatedly planted every spring; this is easier than digging up tender bulbs in fall and storing them over the winter.

Some of the taller summer-blooming bulbs, lilies and *Lycoris*, for example, have naked bottoms. They are happiest when they grow through the outer skirts of such leafy perennials as *Aster × Frikartii* 'Wonder of Staffa', *Coreopsis* 'Early Sunrise' and *Lupinus polyphyllus* 'Russell Hybrids', which allow no distraction from their beauty by hiding the unattractive bottoms of their stems.

Designing with Fall Bulbs

Fall-blooming bulbs also benefit from companionship, but they have to be planned for a little differently. Fall-blooming bulbs are few, and the only temperamental one is *Colchicum*. Unlike spring-blooming bulbs, *Colchicum* and fall crocus send up their foliage in spring. The foliage of fall crocus is short and

grasslike and comes and goes without drawing attention to itself. You need to recognize it to keep from weeding it out of the garden. The *Colchicum*, however, has fat, broad leaves, larger than the largest daffodil leaves. One frenzied fall I planted them in the lawn, duplicating a famous garden's grand scheme on a small plot, but I neglected to make a note for myself. The following spring, forgetting what I had planted in fall, I complained about the large-leaf, overfertilized daffodils that were not blooming and wondered what had possessed me to plant them in the lawn. A visiting gardening friend came to my rescue. She commented on how unsightly *Colchicum* foliage was, waking me from my winter doze to realize my mistake.

It is true they are the most unsightly of plants when dying back in spring. It takes restraint to use only polite language to describe them. I call them "jaundiced," but they are worse than that. With *Colchicum* it is a matter of taking the good with the bad and the ugly. They are the most complicated of bulbs to plant well. Their spring leaves are large, but in fall flowers bloom beautifully on their short stems. If they're planted under tall perennials in spring, the

sickly dying leaves are camouflaged but then come fall, the very beautiful flowers are hidden. A meadow planting would be ideal—plant them among the tall grass and wildflowers to grow up in the spring with their ugly, dying foliage hidden. Then, mow the meadow once in late August, before the flower buds appear. But not having a meadow, I moved them under the creeping phlox (*Phlox subulata*), which blooms in spring and forms a dark green, tightly woven rug before the *Colchicum* awakes. Common sense dictates that it would be difficult for anything to grow up through the phlox's scraggy foliage. But gardening is full of miracles, and over the growing season creeping phlox and *Colchicum* work well together, solving one garden dilemma.

In spring *Colchicum* leaves are still unsightly, but I have massed early summer-blooming perennials nearby to attract attention from this eyesore. As I pass, I walk a little quicker, remembering to look the other way. But in fall, I pause to enjoy the picture of their soft lilac petals lying on a bed of deep green, spiny foliage. It is a sight both dramatic and memorable.

SUMMER BULBS FOR CONTAINERS

Many tender summer-blooming bulbs are easily grown in pots on patios, balconies or terraces. They are easier to grow than many summer flowers and, with little effort, you can bring the

pots indoors to winter over and save them for increased bloom each year.

Climbing lilies, calla lilies and the lower-growing dahlias are excellent choices for full

sun, *Achimenes*, *Caladium* and tuberous begonias are good for shade. Follow the easy potting directions in "Plant Portraits" for each kind. A soilless planting mix, available at nurseries, suits all of them best. These mixes are sterile to prevent soil-borne disease, and they contain nutrients for good bulb growth.

Good drainage is essential, and it is best to plant in a pot with a hole in the bottom. If you place a saucer under the pot, be sure it doesn't impede drainage. Feed potted bulbs regularly with a liquid houseplant fertilizer when they form buds and continue feeding throughout the summer; then, in autumn and before the first frost, move the pots indoors and stop watering in order to induce dormancy. Store the bulbs dry in their pots or dig them up and put them in dry peat moss or vermiculite for the winter. They will keep well at room temperature, between 65° and 75°F. The following spring, repot and divide (page 31), if necessary, and begin the cycle all over again.

TENDER BULBS FOR SUMMER CONTAINERS

Agapanthus (African lily)
Begonia (tuberous begonia)
Caladium (fancy-leafed caladium)
Canna (Indian shot)
Clivia (kafir lily)
Dahlia (dahlia)
Eucomis (pineapple lily)
Galtonia (summer hyacinth)
Gladiolus (gladiola)
Gloriosa (climbing lily)
Hippeastrum (amaryllis)
Ranunculus (Persian buttercup)
Zephyranthes (calla lily)

Stately foliage and a handsome terra-cotta planter give this pixie hybrid lily an unusually formal appearance.

BULBS AS CUT FLOWERS

Having lots of flowers for cutting is a bonus of growing bulbs, especially those that bloom in spring when little else is available for arrangements. Daffodils and hyacinths will carry their delightful fragrance indoors, and tulips can be massed in large bouquets of pleasing colors. Dainty snowdrops and glory-of-the-snow come so early they seem to help push winter on its way; both are charming in miniature arrangements. Dutch iris are elegant in glass vases or as centerpieces, and allium adds a dramatic note when combined with other early summer flowers. Lilies are one of the longer-lasting cut flowers; they will even keep out of water for a few days.

There are a few things to remember when cutting flowers. All bulbs benefit from having their flowers cut, although only a very few will rebloom that season. It halts the production of seed, so energy is conserved for next season's blooms. Be careful, however, to take as few leaves as possible. They are needed to replenish the bulb with stored food for the next year's flowers.

All cut flowers last longer if you condition them immediately after picking by putting the stems in a deep container of lukewarm water and set them in a cool place, out of direct light, for a few hours. This gradually accustoms early spring flowers to the warmer indoor temperatures. Any hollow-stemmed flowers such as daffodil should be sealed as soon as they are picked, by plunging the bottom ½ inch of the stems into boiling water for 30 seconds before conditioning them.

Plant enough bulbs so that you won't be depleting the garden display when you pick flowers for the house. If you have the luxury of a cutting garden, this won't be a problem. If not, perhaps an out-of-the-way area could be set aside for growing bulbs for cutting. Consider a corner of the vegetable garden.

Left: There are many spring bulbs that bloom at the same time and can be cut for lovely, mixed spring bouquets.

Below: Generous plantings of a variety of bulbs ensure a supply of flowers for cutting while leaving others to be enjoyed in the garden bed.

THE BULB PLANTING AND GROWING GUIDE

WHERE TO PLANT

Bulbs are undemanding plants and adapt well to most gardens. One cardinal rule that must be observed: Plant them only in very well-drained soil. Gently sloping sites are ideal because they always enjoy better drainage. Any site where water stands after a rainfall is deadly. If you must plant where the soil is known to remain wet, raise the soil level in the entire bed by 6 to 12 inches, depending on the type of bulbs to be planted. The bulbs must not sit on soggy soil because they will rot, and a raised bed with good, porous soil will solve the problem.

Most bulbs thrive in full sun, but tolerate partial shade if they receive five to six hours of strong light each day. Grape hyacinths, Siberian squill, winter aconite, wood hyacinth, snowdrops and crocus will all grow well in the high, filtered shade of deciduous trees or on the north side of a building. Some, like *Fritillaria* and wood hyacinth, prefer light shade. If they are planted in full sun, mulch the ground to protect the bulbs. Siberian squills flourish in any light, tolerating even deep shade. The "Plant Portraits" chapter will advise on sun requirements.

Soil Preparation

Good soil preparation is the most important step for any gardener. Scrimp and take shortcuts in garden preparation and it will catch up with you later. It is the insurance essential for healthy, productive bulbs. Because most bulbs are left alone to look after themselves for several years, this initial preparation offers the best opportunity to improve the soil and ensure years of top performance. Only in well-prepared, well-drained soil can bulbs continue to increase and multiply over the years.

Bulbs grow best in light, well-drained soil, rich in humus. Very sandy soils and heavy clay soils need lots of added organic matter—compost, peat moss or well-rotted cow manure—to improve the texture. (Never use horse manure in a garden where you will plant bulbs. It is much too rich.) Hybrid tulips are an exception, preferring a sandy soil that is not overly rich in humus. Loose, friable soil beneath a bulb encourages good root growth and promotes adequate drainage. It is a good idea to prepare the soil at least a few inches deeper than the recommended planting depth. The base of the bulb must sit on several inches of properly prepared, nutritious soil.

If you are preparing a garden bed from scratch, rototill or turn over the soil with a spade or shovel to a depth of 12 inches, breaking up any solid clumps. The soil removed from the top of the bed is the most nutritious, the "topsoil."

This showing of spring-blooming bulbs is at once dramatic and natural in appearance.

This you want on the bottom where the bulbs can use it, and the soil from the bottom of the hole goes back on top. Remember: "bottoms up." Spread 2 to 3 inches of peat moss or compost on top of the garden and turn the soil once again to mix it thoroughly. If you don't need to plant your bulbs immediately, water the bed to help it settle. If you can wait a few weeks before planting, that's best.

Very acid soil will benefit from an application of ground limestone. There are several ways to find out the acidity of your soil. Have a soil test made through your local county agricultural agent or your local nursery, make the test yourself with an inexpensive soil kit or use a pH meter at slightly greater cost. The home test kit and pH meter are available from gardening catalogs and at most local gardening centers.

The condition of the soil is measured on a scale of acidity that runs from 1 to 14, which is called the "pH scale." A pH reading tells the gardener whether the soil is acid (1 to 6.5), neutral (6.5 to 7.5) or alkaline (7.5 to 14). Most bulbs like the soil on the acid side of neutral, about 6.5, although anywhere between 6 and 7 will bring good results. Readings at either extreme indicate conditions under which the nutrients in the soil are less available to the plants and the plants are deprived of food.

Bulbs on Arrival

Ideally, bulbs should be planted immediately after you receive them. A bulb, even out of the ground, is a living plant and it

Virginia bluebells complement yellow daffodils. Both will naturalize and increase in number each year.

belongs in the earth, not on a shelf. Spring-blooming bulbs have usually traveled long distances, most from Holland and England to the supplier, before they reach the home gardener.

Order bulbs from a reputable mail-order catalog, like Burpee, where the bulbs have been kept refrigerated until it is time to ship them. If bulbs sit in a nursery, in the sun on a farm stand or on a grocery-store shelf where they are exposed to temperatures above 70°F, they will have diminished bloom or, sadly, no bloom at all.

If you can't plant bulbs on arrival, open the packages so that the air can circulate freely around the bulbs, and keep them in a cool, dry place. Don't leave bulbs in unopened boxes in a heated, moist room where they can begin to grow. Although it's not ideal for those bulbs that should be planted in fall, most can be kept unplanted for several months and planted during a winter thaw. The one bulb that is an exception

is winter aconite. If out of the ground for any length of time, it shrivels. It must be planted immediately upon receipt. The trick for the other bulbs is to keep them dry, dark and cool. The bottom shelf of a refrigerator or a cool room works well. It is best to open the box and spread the bulbs out on a screen or hang them in a perforated paper bag or net onion bag to allow good air circulation. Light, heat and moisture (including humidity in the air) all activate bulb growth. Sometimes a bluish gray, powdery mold collects on the bulbs when they are left too long before planting. It is harmless and can be wiped off with a damp cloth. Discard any bulb that is mushy or has soft spots.

Early Fall Planting of Bulbs

It is important to plant bulbs as early as possible in fall. Early planting gives the bulbs time to establish good root systems

before the freezing weather arrives. The roots will then hold the bulbs in the ground during freezing and thawing. If strong roots are established they will help feed and plump the bulbs. The roots are the bulbs' food lines, through which the plants receive all of their nourishment and moisture from the soil. Although your bulb arrives from the commercial grower force-fed and ready to give beautiful bloom the following year, it will completely deplete itself and will need to be plumped again with food, which is stored for the following year's bloom.

Bulbs that have a very short dormancy (daffodil, crocus and some of the very early spring bulbs, for example) should be planted in September or early October if possible. However, when autumn is just too hectic, I have stored them, successfully sneaking them underground on a thawing January day, to have them bloom half-heartedly and later than usual. (It is better than losing them entirely.) Over the summer they recover any lost luster, blooming well and on time the following year.

If you encounter a snag in your gardening schedule, you can plant your bulbs later than the recommended time, up until the ground freezes. But sometimes, as I learned (particularly in cold climates), late planting means diminished bloom the first year.

One exception to this early planting rule is the tulip family. Tulips are confused when they arrive, having been out of the soil for several weeks or longer, and they are stimulated by moisture, warmth and soil into thinking it's time to bloom. If planted in early fall they will send up top growth rather than sending down roots. If it has time to grow above ground in fall, this top growth will be damaged by winter weather and bloom may be destroyed. If you notice fall top growth, mulch over the tulips sprouts with compost, and if the ground is frozen solid, salt hay or evergreen boughs provide protection through the winter.

Some bulbs, such as snowdrops, are adapted to push up early. Their small, tightly wrapped shoots are unhurt by winter weather. If it snows, all the better. Snow is a good insulator and will protect the bulbs.

Other common causes of premature top growth in fall are too-shallow planting and unseasonably warm and rainy weather (which stimulate growth). Only the very early bulbs (among them snowdrops, winter aconite and glory-of-the-snow) will be unhurt by this. Don't mulch these bulbs in winter—it may kill them by adding to their already-tough job of growing and blooming through frozen ground and, sometimes, snow. They appreciate a mulch in spring after blooming or in the summer, when it has a chance to break down and provide them with nutrients.

Too-shallow planting can cause the bulbs to be baked by summer's scorching sun, and this will dehydrate them during their dormant period. It can also cause them to be heaved out of the ground by winter's alternate freezing and thawing (making them accessible for a rodent's dinner). Finally, too-shallow planting means that the warmed bulbs may send up their foliage too soon (exceptions to this are grape hyacinth and the star-of-bethlehem, whose foliage sprout fully in fall and stay throughout the winter).

Above left: Burpee's 'Cotton Candy' collection of tulips blooms under a tree before its leaves appear in spring.

Above right: 'Red Emperor' is one of the boldest of the fosteriana tulips— one of the earliest blooming tulips.

MAINTENANCE

Bulbs are among nature's most carefree plants, whether in beds or naturalized. Your bulbs will last for many years if you provide adequate moisture during dry spells (especially while foliage ripens) and apply an inch or two of compost (or a slow-release fertilizer) over them in fall. Divide the bulbs if they become crowded. (Tulips develop somewhat differently; refer to the tulip Plant Portrait, pages 74–76, for specifics.)

After your bulbs have bloomed, their leaves must mature for three to five weeks to build up the bulb's energy and food supply for flowering the next season. When the leaves have yellowed and dried, you can cut them off at the base. Ripening foliage of some of the larger bulbs may detract from the appearance of your garden. Refer to the design tips on pages 19–24 for ways to interplant them with spreading perennials, groundcovers or annuals to conceal the fading leaves.

Daffodil foliage is very slow

Primroses bloom under snowflakes on the banks of the stream.

to mature. It is better not to resort to the old-fashioned custom of tying, bending, braiding or scrunching the leaves together with rubber bands to make them tidy. (I personally can't imagine having that much time on my hands.) The leaves are damaged and bruised when handled this way and are deprived of the sunlight so important to their development. Fussing with foliage is one of the main reasons why bulbs do not return in the garden. Conveniently, the foliage of small spring-flowering bulbs usually withers quickly and is rarely noticed or considered unsightly.

Although it is essential to allow bulb foliage to ripen, the flower heads may be removed soon after blooming to prevent seed production and thus help the bulbs conserve their energy for the next year's bloom.

Composting

A garden is only as good as its soil. Composting for yearly replenishing of the nutrients in the soil is the single most important step a gardener can take toward building a beautiful garden. Without nutrients plants can't thrive. Nature, however, has made it easy. All the gardener needs to do is follow nature's lead and work with it. A simple pile of leaves left behind the garage to decompose is perfectly adequate compost. The leaves will break down over the period of a year into a fine, black humus, which can be shoveled onto the garden each

fall. Nutrients in the compost will be carried by rainwater through the soil to the plants' roots and will be readily available in spring when needed by the bulbs.

Once you see the results of adding compost to your garden, you will not be willing to wait a year for your dead leaves to break down. There are almost as many different methods of composting as there are gardeners. The purpose of all the different methods is to speed up decomposition. A pile left standing behind the garage to decompose on its own is the slowest method of producing compost. If leaves are layered in a compost bin, alternating with an inch of soil and a sprinkling of ground limestone, and watered thoroughly once in fall, the many organisms from the soil will help the leaves break down faster. Composting can be further speeded up if the pile is turned over with a spade or shovel every week or two. Ready-made compost bins are designed to hold in heat, and that speeds the process even more.

My preference is to rake the leaves in fall and shred them on the spot, returning them directly to the garden. Shredded leaves are attractive as a mulch, give the plants some winter protection and bring them nutrients in spring (shredded leaves break down more quickly). This eliminates the steps of bagging and moving the leaves and carrying them back to the garden in the summer. I do keep a compost pile for garden cleanup that is filled with excess leaves, vegetable peelings, grass clippings and other material gathered over the entire year, not just in fall.

Mulching

Mulch is a valuable aid for conserving moisture and protecting the bulbs from the high heat of summer. A 2- to 4-inch cover of pine needles, shredded leaves or compost will keep the ground moist, minimize weeds and protect bulbs from summer heat. Most important, a winter mulch will prevent alternate thaws and freezing that can heave newly planted bulbs out of the ground during the winter. Apply your mulch after the ground has frozen to keep it from thawing until the arrival of spring. Groundcovers are "living mulches," affording the same protection and creating a handsome backdrop for your bulbs.

Fertilizing

Hardy bulbs, especially those in established colonies and those growing in sandy soils, should have soil nutrients replaced yearly. The best way to fertilize bulbs is to put an inch or two of compost on the area where your bulbs are planted every year. This means you can avoid the use of a chemical fertilizer. The nitrogen in chemical fertilizers breaks down quickly and leaches with the rainwater through the soil to pollute our water. Earthworms, the capable creatures who help do our tilling, can't live in a soil with chemical fertilizers.

If you feel you need more nutrients for your plants, use only a slow-release fertilizer; it will break down slowly, staying in the top portion of the soil—where your plants can use it. The best fertilizer for bulbs is Holland Bulb Booster. Apply it in early fall when roots start to grow and work into the surface of the soil. Holland Bulb Booster, developed at North Carolina State University, is formulated to release the correct balance of nutrients required by bulbs over the entire growing season. It is more effective than bone meal, and bulbs bloom better and rebloom longer. Rain will carry it down to the bulbs as they begin to root. Because Holland Bulb Booster releases nutrients slowly, it feeds bulbs for their entire growth cycle, right through spring. You may use a standard slow-release 5-10-5 commercial fertilizer instead, but it will not be the equivalent of a completely balanced meal for bulbs. Bone meal, although good for bulbs, has the same problem. It is effective sprinkled in the hole before planting, where it will be available for the roots; sprinkled on the ground, it will simply stay there. The smell of bone meal also attracts dogs and other animals who might dig up your plantings.

Division

Plantings of daffodil, *Fritillaria* and most small bulbs can be left undisturbed for years. But some bulbs, multiply rapidly and eventually become so crowded that they exhaust the soil around them. Small, sparse blossoms in a mature clump of bulbs is a sure sign that your hardy bulbs need to be divided. This may be done right after the foliage has turned yellow. Dig up the bulb clump, taking care not to injure the bulbs. Break the clump apart and replant the larger bulbs where you want a good show of flowers next year. The smaller, less mature bulbs may be planted in an inconspicuous place where they will grow for a year or two until they are big enough to bloom. Some gardeners allow newly dug, divided bulbs to dry in a cool, dark place for a few days before replanting them. This is to reduce spoilage, because it gives the cut surfaces of the bulbs a chance to "heal."

What goes in the compost pile:

Remember that the smaller the pieces are, the faster they will decompose.

Shredded or whole fall leaves (first drag a lawn mower back and forth over leaves to shred, or use a leaf shredder)
Shredded bark (you'll need a wood chipper for this)
Shredded twigs
Fresh vegetable and fruit peelings
Grass cuttings
Tea leaves
Coffee grounds
Well-rotted horse or cow manure
Eggshells
Cut flowers
Pine needles

What not to put in the compost pile:

Cooked food
Weeds with seedpods
Raw fish and animal remains (good compost, but they attract mice and other small animals)
Diseased plants (the disease will spread)
Any plant material that has been treated with a herbicide or pesticide within three weeks of possible use for compost

To divide bulbs, gently break them apart being, careful to keep the roots intact.

Corms, tiny roots and all, are gently removed from the mother bulb for replanting.

Transplanting Bulbs

Eventually, no matter how carefully you selected the positions for your various bulbs, there comes a time for transplanting. Perhaps a vigorous clump of daffodils is now exactly where you don't want it to be. Or a pretty clump of snowdrops is blooming merrily in a spot earmarked for a new shrub. Can you move the errant bulbs, and if so, when? Common wisdom is that spring-blooming bulbs should be planted in autumn, but the period immediately following spring bloom is the right time for transplanting and division. Moving bulbs in spring gives you the opportunity to assess carefully the balance of color and placement in your garden. As the blooms fade, simply dig the clump, divide it if you like and then plant it in a new location, retaining as much of the soil around the bulbs as possible. Water well, and allow the foliage to mature and die before removing it.

A formal planting of tulips and hyacinth will have to be replanted every year because these bulbs are not reliable—you'll have fewer bulbs that bloom each year, and gradually over a few years, they will disappear. To increase they require perfect drainage and dry summer conditions, demands that aren't often met. They become unsightly after blooming but it will not hurt them if they are carefully moved to another spot until their foliage dies down. They can be left all summer and replanted in fall, or they can be dug up and stored over the summer in a cool, dark place. Fall is the time to plant new bulbs only because that is when they are dormant and available for purchase.

Spring is the easiest time for a home gardener to move bulbs into a better position or to divide overcrowded areas because this is when it's easiest to see where the bulbs are and to dig without damaging them. Dividing bulbs in fall is a dangerous business. Stabbing into the ground with a pitch fork in the general area where you thought the spring bulbs bloomed has caused the demise of many a bulb, impaled or sliced up.

Storing Hardy Bulbs over the Summer

In the days of more formal plantings of bulbs, when various colored tulips were used to spell out a name or create an elaborate design, bulbs were so closely planted that nothing could be grown in the bed with them. The gardener could not be assured of equal results the following year. Consequently, the tulips were dug up after blooming and heeled into a trench, hidden from view, while the foliage died back unseen by garden guests. After the foliage matured and was removed, the bulbs were stored for the summer and later replanted in a cutting garden to provide blooms for the house while the formal garden was replanted with newly purchased bulbs.

You can dig up and store your hardy bulbs over the summer for fall replanting. Good air circulation and moderate temperatures are required. Store bulbs in net bags or old nylon stockings in quantities of no more than two dozen per bag, and hang them in a dry place. The ideal storage temperature is 65° to 70°F. Check them regularly and remove any that begin to rot, to prevent others from going bad.

Daffodils, so frequently enjoyed in casual settings— cascading down hillsides, planted in drifts—lend their light-hearted charm to this more formal planting.

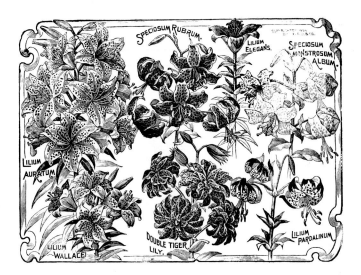

Propagating Lilies

Lilies reproduce in many ways and are very easy to propagate. Lilium tigrinum and L. umbellatum double every year, and if not divided they will deplete their blooms. L. bulbiferum develops tiny bulblets in the leaf axils, where the leaves join the stems, and these can be gently removed and planted for new bulbs. For some lilies, stem cuttings can be taken and propagated.

Most lilies resemble artichokes with their many swollen scales. The most common means of propagating is to remove a few of the bulbs' scales and grow them on to form new bulbs. Up to half of the scales can be removed without any harm to the bulb. The tricky part is that the scales need to be removed while the lily is flowering or just after it has finished. This means you must carefully dig up the whole bulb, remove the scales and replant immediately, or dig a hole alongside the bulb and remove a few scales without digging up the bulb. Decayed or withered scales are not viable. If you remove the whole bulb, keep it out of the soil for only a few minutes. Avoid working midday in the strong summer sun. The bulb must retain its moisture.

Each scale planted will produce bulblets, which in turn can be planted in the garden the following spring. Use a kitchen food-storage bag filled with a thoroughly damp, but not soggy, soilless mix. The plastic bag will retain the moisture. (If the bag dries out, your scales will die.) Lay the bag flat and insert the fat, bottom end of each scale into the mix. The pointed end of the scales should be visible above the surface of the mix and through the plastic. Seal the bag and cut a small opening in the center of the top to allow air circulation and prevent mildew. Keep the bag in a 70° to 80°F place for six to eight weeks or until bulblets the size of peas are visible on the base of the scales. Move to a cool place such as a cold frame, unheated garage or basement, where the temperature will remain between 35° and 45°F for two to three months. Lilies need a cold, dormant period to induce growth. Next, plant into pots with a good potting mix and continue to grow. In spring, gently separate the bulblets from the scales, keeping any roots with the bulblet. The scales will be depleted, so discard them. Plant the bulbs into the garden as you would any full-size lily bulb of the same species.

Forcing Bulbs

Theoretically, all bulbs can be brought into bloom indoors ("forced") ahead of their normal schedule. Practically, however, some bulbs are easier to force than others. Crocus, hyacinth and most daffodil force well. Remember that bulbs are easiest to force when you time them to bloom fairly close to their natural schedule; the earliest flowering tulips and other bulbs will be more satisfactory indoors than later-blooming varieties.

The forcing process must reproduce, in a short period of time, the effect the climatic changes would have produced on the bulbs had they been left in the ground over the winter. It takes time and frequent tending, but the result is beautiful flowers indoors at a time when flowers outdoors are few.

Tender bulbs are those that grow outdoors only in frost-free areas of the South, Southwest and Pacific Coast, where they may be left in the ground year 'round. Elsewhere in the country they make good indoor plants. The tender bulbs are forced somewhat differently than the hardy bulbs of northern gardens. The exotic flowers of *Freesia*, *Ranunculus*, calla lilies and amaryllis, among the tender bulbs, provide an exquisite complement to other houseplants.

Crocus blooming in a delft planter.

Growing Tulips as Perennials

In order to maintain the same number of blooms the second year, a tulip bulb must replace itself with at least one bulb of equal size and several bulbs of lesser size. The mother bulb dies. Much of the nutrients needed for this increased mass of bulbs must come from compost, well-rotted cow manure or slow-release fertilizer added to the soil. The soil must remain light and well drained. Failure to provide nutrients in the soil the first year results in plants with slightly paler green foliage, moderately smaller leaves and a large reduction in the mass of daughter bulbs produced. These effects carry into the second and subsequent years, leading to smaller flowers and poorer plant appearance.

The pH level is the first concern in tulip culture. Tulips tolerate a broad range; 5.4 to 7.3 is preferred. A pH lower than 5.4 invites the possibility of calcium deficiency. A slow-release fertilizer should be applied in fall. Over the winter it will work its way down through the soil to where the bulb can use it when it wakes from its dormancy. Bulbs should not be fertilized at or after flowering in spring. At this time the nutrients are of little, if any, benefit to the plants; they won't have had enough time to work their way toward the bulbs' roots before the bulbs go into dormancy.

Deep planting of tulips has notable advantages and is well worth the extra effort of preparing the soil deeply. When tulips are set 9 to 10 inches deep, instead of the usual 4 to 6 inches, their blooming is prolonged. Because deep planting discourages the bulbs from splitting (reproducing themselves), the bulbs will continue to bloom, with larger flowers, for several seasons. (Daughter bulbs don't bloom immediately.) Deeper-than-usual planting also allows you to plant annuals or shallow-rooted perennials over your bulbs after they have died back, because the bulbs lie below the digging depth of the soil. For deep planting, remember that good drainage is essential.

Tête-à-Tête Narcissus bloom in a terra—cotta bowl.

Forcing Hardy Bulbs

The procedure for forcing hardy bulbs to bloom indoors ahead of their outdoor schedule is fairly simple and very rewarding. Hyacinth and paperwhite *Narcissus* are perhaps the easiest to force, and tulip is the most challenging. Among the tulip varieties, the easiest to force are the early singles and early doubles.

Planting in Pots

All spring-flowering bulbs should be potted up in late September or early October. Forcing will take about 12 weeks for the early-blooming bulbs (crocus, snowdrops, daffodil) and about 16 weeks for the later bulbs (tulip). By planting many kinds and carefully timing their bloom, you can have indoor color from late December through April.

The quality of the bulb determines its performance when forced. Always use healthy, firm bulbs, large for their size, that are guaranteed to grow and bloom. Any container from a clay pot to a china bowl will work. The important consideration is that the container be clean and permit good drainage. The ideal size is a container that is half as high as it is wide, providing more planting space for a cluster of bulbs.

The kind and size of the bulbs will determine the height of the container. For the best display, plant as many bulbs as the pot will hold, leaving ½ inch of space between the bulbs and around the edge of the pot. Most bulbs look best when planted in groups of 6 to 12 bulbs per pot, all of the same kind or variety. Hyacinth looks well planted either individually in 4- to 5-inch pots, or in groups. A group of 2 or 3 large daffodil bulbs, or 6 hybrid tulip bulbs, or 12 crocus corms will fill a 6-inch pot. Dense planting is recommended for the small bulbs.

Place a piece of broken pottery

or an inch of pebbles in the bottom of the pot over the drainage hole (add a shallow layer of gravel or pebbles next, if starting with broken pottery). Half-fill the pot with a good potting mix. Set the bulbs on the soil (be sure the tops are pointing up!), with the tops just below the rim of the pot; do not press the bulbs into the soil. Add more soil until only the tips of the bulbs are visible. Small bulbs can be covered with ½ inch of soil.

Water the pot thoroughly, either from the top or by immersing the entire pot in a tub of water. Let the excess water drain off. Label each pot, noting the kind and variety (or color) of the bulbs and the date of planting.

For this first stage of the forcing process, store the pots of bulbs in a cool, dark place. Any cool (35° to 45°F), frost-free location is suitable for good root development: an unheated attic, porch or attached garage; a ventilated, darkened cold frame; a root cellar or a spare refrigerator. If necessary, set boxes, pots or burlap over your potted bulbs to keep them dark during this period. Keep the soil barely damp; check periodically and water only when the soil is nearly dry.

After 8 to 12 weeks of cold temperatures, the bulbs should have a good root mass. When the top sprouts are 2 to 3 inches high, move the bulbs to a warmer location. This will force the bloom. (I have forgotten bulbs from time to time and brought them out when the stems were 6 inches high and a jaundiced yellow. One day of sunlight will restore their healthy green color.)

When potted bulbs are brought out and set in a sunny window, I like to sprinkle grass seed on top of the soil and between the tops of the bulbs. The grass germinates in a week and grows quickly if kept moist. By the time the bulbs bloom, the bare soil is no longer visible, and the green grass completes the beauty of the blossoms.

Some bulbs have been "precooled" by the grower in order to be ready to force as soon as they are received. They do not need the 8 to 12 weeks of root development because that's already been accomplished at the grower's. Precooled hyacinth, crocus and tulip bulbs (the most commonly available) can be potted just as described for other hardy bulbs; precooled hyacinth and crocus may be grown in soil or water. Follow the specific recommendations shipped with your precooled bulbs.

For best results, the bulbs should be exposed gradually to warmer temperatures and brighter light. Bring the pots to a bright, cool (55° to 65°F) room. (You can stagger bloom by not bringing all the pots out at once.) Keep them out of direct sunlight. Water frequently and feed weekly with a half-strength solution of houseplant fertilizer. Turn the pots every day or so to keep the flower stems straight. In a week or two, the stems will elongate and the buds will become plump. When the foliage and the buds are well developed, move the pots to a bright, sunny window; temperatures can be somewhat warmer. As the flowers open, you can prolong their bloom by moving the pots away from direct sunlight to a cooler place.

Care of Easter Lilies after Blooming

Lilium longiflorum, *commonly called the "Easter lily," does not grow satisfactorily outdoors in the northern states. It is tender and even when it survives the winter, it does not seem as permanent or long-lived as other garden lilies. L. candidum, the Madonna lily, is hardy and permanent with pure white flowers, smaller and more flaring than those of the Easter lily; it is often forced for Easter and is a good garden plant.*

When your lilies have ceased blooming, leave the bulbs in the pots, giving them full sunshine and plenty of water to keep them growing. As the weather becomes warmer, sink the pots outside in the soil to the depth of the rim. This helps prevent the pots from drying out and baking in the sun. Water the pots regularly until August, when growth will gradually cease and the leaves will gradually become yellow and wither. Water should be gradually withheld as the top dries off. When the stem is dead, the pots should be dug up and stored in a cool, frost-free place where they will not dry out entirely until it is time to repot.

In October shake the dry earth off the bulbs and put them in clean pots. A suitable soil is two-thirds potting soil and one-third dried cow manure (both available in bags from nurseries). Put broken crockery or pebbles in the bottom of the pot with 2 inches of soil above them; barely cover the bulbs with soil. Later, as the bulbs begin to sprout, add more soil for the stem roots to run in. Keep the pots in a cool cellar, or plunged into the soil in a sheltered spot outside and covered with a mulch. Water as needed to keep the soil barely moist, until the roots are well formed. At this point, the plants may be brought into the house. After the roots are established, the pots should be given sunlight and watered regularly until the bulbs finish blooming, and the cycle is repeated.

'Ziva' *paperwhite daffodils are forced to bloom indoors in a Delft bowl.*

Hyacinth bulbs may be grown in hyacinth glasses suspended above water so the water just touches the bottom of the bulb.

After flowering, cut off the flower stems and move the pots into direct sunlight. Keep them growing until the foliage fully matures and then withers. Don't pull off leaves until they are absolutely dead. Store the bulbs, still in their pots, in a cool, dry place until late summer or early fall, when they can be planted in the garden. Do not try to force the same bulbs again indoors. Forcing weakens the bulbs and you will have unsatisfactory bloom if you try to force them repeatedly. Back in the garden, they can return to their natural schedule, and their temporarily diminished bloom will not be as noticeable among the other garden plants.

The Water Method

This simplest of all methods of forcing crocus, hyacinth and 'Soleil d'Or' *Narcissus* and paperwhite *Narcissus* is an old-time favorite of children and adults alike. Decide when you want your bulbs to flower. Bulbs started at 10-day intervals will provide a sequence of bloom for many weeks or months. Store the bulbs in perforated paper bags and keep them in a cool, dark, dry place until you are ready to use them; the bottom shelf of a refrigerator is fine for hyacinth and crocus, but is too cold for daffodil.

Paperwhite *Narcissus* will bloom four to six weeks after you start them; for Christmas bloom, start the bulbs in mid-November. 'Soleil d'Or' *Narcissus* usually need about six weeks as well. Hyacinth requires a longer period, six to eight weeks, to establish good roots. Crocus needs a much more gradual transition from dark to light and must be kept cool until buds rise from the leaves, so do not expect flowers before the end of January if bulbs are started mid-November.

To grow bulbs in water, select a container about twice as deep as the bulbs, and fill it ½ to ¾ full with clean pebbles, marbles, gravel or coarse sand. Place the bulbs on top, pointed end up, and fill the container with water until it just touches the base of the bulbs. (A piece of ordinary charcoal tucked under water among the pebbles will keep it fresh.) Fill the spaces between the bulbs with additional gravel or sand to hold them firmly upright. Set the dish of bulbs in a dark, cool (50° to 60°F), well-ventilated spot, such as a cool closet or basement. Leave them until you see a good root mass develop, usually within two to four weeks; the sprouts should be 2 to 3 inches. Check the water level occasionally to make sure the roots are always immersed; roots die quickly if deprived of water. Move the dish to a cool location with strong, indirect light (such as a north window) for three or four days. Finally, move it into full sunlight. Once the flowers open, you can prolong their bloom by moving the bulbs to a cooler place out of direct sunlight. Discard the bulbs after they have bloomed. The water method zaps all their energy, and they will not recover, even if planted into the garden.

Narcissus and hyacinth grown by this method usually need staking to look their best when in flower. Support them with sticks inserted into the pebbles or sand as inconspicuously as possible and make a corral for the weak stems by looping green string loosely around each of the sticks. Small metal hoops especially designed for staking small plants and bulbs are commercially available from florists and some nurseries.

Hyacinth and crocus may also be grown by simply suspending the bulb in a glass of water. Specially designed glasses for these bulbs are available, but you may use any tapered glass or jar that holds the bulb above the water. Fill the glass so the water just touches the bottom of the bulb. Change the water every couple of weeks, taking care to maintain the correct water level. Keep the bulbs in a cool, dark place until the lower portion of the glass fills with roots, then move it gradually into greater light and warmth. Discard the bulb after flowering.

Forcing Tender Bulbs

Tender bulbs, those that grow outdoors only in warm, frost-free climates, provide striking, colorful and often fragrant flowers for indoor pots to brighten northern winters. Most tender bulbs do best in a moderately cool (55 to 65°F), sunny place in your home or greenhouse. (See "Plant Portraits" for individual plants' needs. *Anemone, Freesia* and *Ranunculus* need cool temperatures to force successfully indoors for winter and spring bloom.) An unheated, enclosed sunporch may be ideal; otherwise, grow the bulbs in the coolest room that offers a sunny window, and bring the potted bulbs into the warmer living areas only when they bloom.

All the tender bulbs need frequent watering during their period of active growth, plus a weekly application of a good houseplant fertilizer at half-strength. They thrive in a moist atmosphere, so increase the humidity by placing the pots on trays of pebbles partially covered with water; water shouldn't touch the pot but is intended to increase humidity around the pot. Rotate the pots when you water them to keep the stems growing straight. When potting, provide good drainage by placing a layer of pebbles or gravel in the bottom of the pot, and use a rich, porous growing medium.

Pots of tender bulbs may be sunk up to their rims in the garden after they have bloomed and after all danger of spring frost. This is an easy way to care for them while the foliage ripens. Water them during dry spells to keep the roots from drying out. Well before the first frost in fall, lift the pots and stack them in a cool, dry, out-of-the-way place where they will not freeze. Gradually discontinue watering as the foliage withers and the bulbs become dormant.

A 6-inch pot or bulb pan will hold six to twelve bulbs, depending on their size. Plant them in a good potting mix, placing them so the tops of the bulbs are barely covered. Water well and place the pots in a cool, dark, frost-free place (preferably 40° to 50°F) for several weeks while roots develop. Water sparingly at this time. When top growth begins, move the pots to a moderately cool (50° to 60°F), sunny window; water freely and feed weekly with houseplant fertilizer at half-strength.

After the flowers have faded, remove their stems. Gradually discontinue watering the plants as the foliage withers and the bulbs become dormant. Then place the pots on their sides in a cool, dry place. Leave the bulbs in their pots until fall, when they can be shaken from the dry soil and repotted. Although the cycle can be started again, we've found that best results come from starting with new bulbs each year, as forcing weakens the bulbs. Some bulbs need support to keep the flower stems from bending while in bloom. See page 36 for techniques.

TENDER BULBS FOR FORCING

Anemone coronaria (anemone)
Freesia (freesia)
Hippeastrum (amaryllis)
Ranunculus (Persian buttercup)
Scilla peruviana (Peruvian scilla)
Zantedeschia (calla lily)

PLANT PORTRAITS

The most popular and readily available bulbs are described in the pages that follow. Under each entry, many different varieties are listed to help you choose which are best for your garden. They are listed under their botanical (Latin) names and cross-referenced by their common names. This is to avoid confusion because several plants can have the same common name, and one plant is known by various common names in different parts of the country. Every known plant has a first name, the genus (indicated by the first Latin word), a grouping of plants with similar characteristics. Every plant has a second name, too, the species (the second Latin word), which further identifies shared qualities of lesser importance. Using botanical names is the one way to be sure of having the correct cultural information.

PLANT PORTRAIT KEY

Here is a guide to the symbols and terms used throughout this section.

Latin name of the bulb is in boldface italic type.

Phonetic pronunciation of the Latin name is in parentheses.

Common name of the bulb is in boldface type.

The average hours of sun needed per day is indicated by symbols. The first symbol is what the bulb prefers, but the plant is adaptable to all conditions listed.

○ *Sun*—Six hours or more of direct sunlight per day. What you remember as a shady spot may well be very sunny before the trees leaf-out and be a perfect spot for spring bulbs.

◑ *Part shade*—Three to six hours of direct sunlight per day.

● *Shade*—Two hours or less of direct sunlight.

Symbols for:
   ❦ *Long-lasting cut flower*
   ✿ *Fragrant blooms or leaves*
   ❀ *Long bloomer—a month or longer*

T—Tender bulb, plants that are killed by the first frost.

H—Hardy bulb, plants that can survive freezing weather. Check the zone listings to see how far north the bulbs are hardy.

Native American are the plants that were growing on the American continent when the pilgrims arrived. Many plants that are native to

Small bulbs such as glory-of-the-snow and miniature 'Tête-à-Tête' daffodils can be tucked in crevices and between rocks.

America are also native to other countries around the world.

Grade of difficulty describes bulbs that take the least amount of care are identified as "easy." These plants are a good choice for beginning gardeners or gardeners with little time.

Seasons of bloom: SP = spring, SU = summer, F = fall, W = winter; E = early, L = late, i.e., ESP = early spring

Zones: Check "The USDA Plant Hardiness Map" (pages 88–89), based on average annual temperatures for each area—or zone—of the United States to see what zone you live in. Every plant portrait lists the zones best for that plant.

Heights are for normal growth, but bulbs with very fertile soil could grow taller and, conversely, bulbs with poor growing conditions could be shorter.

Cultural information explains plants' preferences for soil and care for optimal growing.

Acidanthera murielae

Agapanthus *species planted with impatiens and lobelia*

Acidanthera (a-si-DAN-ther-a) **peacock orchid, H,** easy. ○ ✿.

Zones: 7 to 10

Height: 1½ to 3½ feet

Colors: White, with chocolate brown or red to purple centers

Characteristics: The delightfully scented flowers are blotched with blackish purple in the center, which makes them look like great butterflies swaying above sword-shaped leaves. The flowers bloom for two months or longer from the end of summer into fall, the blooms opening in sequence from the bottom of the flower spike to the top. Plant *Acidanthera* in groups of a dozen or more and place it near the house or on a terrace where you can enjoy its fragrance. It is good for cutting. Remove faded flowers to promote branching and bring even more flowers. A native from Ethiopia to South Africa, the peacock orchid is related to the *Gladiolus* family, and its culture is similar. Peacock orchid also makes a good potted plant.

Cultural Information: Plant it in spring after all danger of frost, spacing the corms 6 inches apart and 3 to 4 inches deep. For Zone 6 and other northern zones, start the corms indoors in pots or in a cold frame a month or more before the nights remain between 50° and 60°F.

Lift the corms from the garden in fall after the leaves have browned and cut the stems back to within 2 inches of the corm. Store them indoors over winter. In warmer zones where they are left in the ground over the winter, divide the corms in early spring every three to four years. They can be propagated by removing the tiny corms from the base of the mother corm. Planted in fertile soil and grown for two seasons, the new corms will reach flowering size.

Uses: Potted plant, flower garden, cutting.

Aconite, winter; see *Eranthis*

Adder's tongue; see *Erythronium*

African lily; see *Agapanthus*

Agapanthus (ag-a-PAN-thus) **African lily, blue lily of the Nile, T,** easy, SU. ○ ◖ ▮ ✿

Zones: 9 to 10 for evergreen varieties, 7 to 10 for deciduous varieties

Height: 12 to 30 inches

Colors: Blue, white

Characteristics: The blue lily of the Nile comes from southeast Africa and nowhere near the river Nile. (Perhaps the name indicates the route it took to reach European countries, where there are records of its cultivation as early as 1679.) The leathery, strap-shaped, arching leaves reach out from the base of the stem. The naked flower stalks loosely hold globes of graceful, funnel-shaped blooms. Each blossom is between 1 and 4 inches long.

Agapanthus campanulatus is a deciduous variety, losing its leaves in the winter. At 24 inches tall it is very showy, with 12 to 30 flowers in each globe. 'Peter Pan' is a good dwarf variety, 12 to 18 inches tall with dark blue flowers. The dwarf varieties are good accents for rock gardens. In California and the Southwest it is very attractive informally planted outdoors in irregular sweeps. In northern climates it is best grown in wooden tubs rather than terracotta pots because its expanding roots can break the pottery. It can remain for several years in the same container and needs to be repotted only when flowering diminishes.

Cultural Information: Agapanthus prefers fertile, loamy soil—not soggy, but moist; never allow the plant to dry out completely. It needs minimal attention when grown outdoors. In northern zones, store the plant in its tub in a light place, with a cool temperature between 40° and 50°F, to induce dormancy. Too much warmth can be harmful, stimulating new growth. Gradually withhold water, keeping the soil nearly dry. In March move the pot to a warmer place and resume watering generously. *Agapanthus* tends to bloom more freely when its roots are crowded and it is best to disturb the roots as little as possible. It should be lifted, divided and replanted in newly prepared and enriched soil when blooming deteriorates. Propagation is easiest by division. Remove the roots from the pot, wash off the soil with a hose and carefully separate the roots into smaller pieces, each with one or more crowns or shoots. Then replant the roots in good potting soil.
Uses: Cutting, groundcover, potted plant.

Allium (AL-ee-um) **giant allium, flowering onion, yellow allium, H,** easy, SP, F. ○ 🌡

Zones: 4 to 10 (*A. giganteum* and *A. neapolitanum* 6 to 10)
Height: 6 inches to 5 feet
Colors: Purple, yellow, white, blue, lavender
Characteristics: Allium is a member of the onion family but it reminds you of this only from time to time, releasing its onion breath if leaves are bent or crushed. There are hundreds of species of *Allium* from far-flung parts of the globe—North America, Europe, Asia, North Africa and Mexico. Alliums come in all heights, from small to giant, with flower heads made up of blooms 2 to 10 inches across. All varieties bloom for only a few weeks, but they offer a choice of spring, summer or fall bloom. They are all similar in their behavior and appearance, and all are excellent for cutting. (Don't worry about their onion breath; it will disappear if they stand in cool water for 10 minutes before arranging.)

No matter what their size, the long, broad leaves tend to be land lovers, hugging the ground. Each plant sends up a bare stem, thin and straight, carrying a full, rounded head of flowers. The dried flower heads are attractive and can be left on the plant for garden interest or brought in for use in winter flower arrangements. Flower heads may be left on the plant to dry, or they can be removed at the height of bloom and hung upside down in a dry, dark closet where they will dry without damage from wind, rain or sun.

A. giganteum, the giant allium, is handsome and stately with huge balls of purple flowers. Each ball is formed by numerous 6-inch, star-shaped blossoms and sits on 4- to 5-foot stems. This plant stands out in the garden and can look gangly if not planted at the back of the border behind 2- to 3-foot-high plants. The giant allium blooms in late June and early July. Because of its height and the weight of its flowers, the plant may need staking. (If planted

Allium aflatunense
shown with chives

Allium Moly *(yellow) with* Allium oreophilum

Allium karataviense

where it is protected from strong winds, this may not be necessary.)

A. Moly, yellow allium, is from southwest Europe, where it was reputed to bring good luck to whoever grew it. Its bright yellow, starry blooms face up and are positioned close together on 10-inch-high stems. A pair of leaves accompanies the flowers and is similar to those of tulips. Blooms appear from May to June and may last longer than three weeks in light shade.

A. oreophilum, originally from Asia, has purplish pink florets similar to those of *A. Moly*, but grows only 6 inches high. My favorite is the Russian-born *A. caeruleum* (known also as *A. azureum*), the blue garlic, with its compact, 1-inch balls of clear cornflower blue flowers, some with penciled lines through the middle of the petals. It blooms on 2-foot stems in June and is good for naturalizing in groups and for use in bouquets.

The drumstick allium (*A. sphaerocephalum*) is aptly named. Its ball-shaped heads are 1¾ inches across with reddish purple, bell-like blossoms. It is 24 inches high and blooms from late May into June.

A. neapolitanum is the white-flowering allium, known for its pleasant fragrance; it isn't as hardy as other family members.

The strange-looking *A. karataviense* from Turkey is a curiosity, unusual for its broad, arching, blue-gray leaves—the most prominent characteristic. The flowers are a washed-out white tinged with a dusty pink and are arranged in lacy globes.

The delicate, pinkish lavender *A. pulchellum* is 1 to 1½ feet tall, blooms in mid-July and sets seed abundantly.

All alliums can be naturalized in informal clumps or scattered between and around perennial flowers. Some self-sow with abandon. To avoid this, cut off the faded flower heads before the seeds form.

Cultural Information: The soil for alliums should be light loam, moist but well drained. Plant 2 to 3 times as deep as the diameter of the bulbs. Bulbs are spaced 4 to 18 inches apart depending on their height. They need normal moisture throughout the growing season. When growing in Zones 4 and 5, use a winter mulch of hay or wood chips to control alternate freezing and thawing. When the bulbs are crowded, they produce foliage only, an announcement that it is time for them to be divided. Allium lasts for years and multiplies freely.

Uses: Bedding, cutting, background, edging, rock garden, naturalizing, drying.

Alstroemeria (al-stree-MEER-ee-a) **Peruvian lily, H,** moderate, SU. ○ ◐ 🌡 ✿
Zones: 7 to 10
Height: 1 to 4 feet
Colors: Orange, yellow, lilac, pink, red, white streaked with purple
Characteristics: Another case of mistaken identity, *Alstroemeria* is nicknamed "the Peruvian lily" but it is really from Chile or Brazil. It is a prolific bloomer, with clusters of up to 50 blossoms. The blossoms are 1½ to 2 inches wide and resemble the flowers of daylilies. It blooms from early spring to midsummer. Often, two of the five petals are streaked with brown or green. A whorl of 3-to 4-inch leaves provides a collar directly below the flowers.

When harvesting *Alstroemeria* for cut flowers, pull the flower stems out of the ground rather than cutting them, to avoid root rot. Cut off the white part of the stem (the underground portion) before you place it in water. Make a slit ½ inch up the stem to increase water flow.

This temperamental plant can thrive like a weed or show no growth for years. The fleshy root is sensitive to transplanting. The Peruvian lily is rarely seen in gardens today for many reasons. The established rhizomes, originally planted about 6 inches below the surface, make their way lower over time, ending up 18 or more inches under the ground. At this depth, although they are drought resistant, they are hard to move (you practically have to call in a bulldozer). Some varieties have a long dormancy period, eight or nine months, which leaves unsightly bare ground when they

Alstroemeria *species*

die back; pick better varieties, or give these varieties a space of their own or grow them in pots. They need staking or they will have a trampled appearance after a windy or rainy day. Most of the flowers are not fragrant. *Alstroemeria caryophyllaea* (Zones 8 to 10) is one of the few sweetly scented.

In northern zones *Alstroemeria* can be grown in pots. Where summers are exceptionally hot, light shade is welcome. *A. aurantiaca*, from Chile, is the hardiest variety but offers less variety of color, just orange to yellow. The foliage stays until after frost. *Alstroemeria* can be very invasive so be careful to plant it where it won't crowd out nearby plants. It can be divided every three years or transplanted, but if even a small bit of fibrous root is left in the ground it may sprout.

Cultural Information: Plant the dormant fleshy roots of *Alstroemeria* in early spring or fall, 8 inches apart and 6 to 9 inches deep in loose, light, fast-draining soil heavily enriched with compost to feed its voracious appetite. This heavy feeder depletes a nutritious soil quickly. It needs full sun and shelter from dry spring winds. Water regularly as soon as the first shoots appear. Stems are delicate, so either grow them through an upright plant they can lean on (*Coreopsis*, for example) or use canes for support. In September, when the foliage disappears, cover the ground with clumps of straw or coarse pine bark for the first few years until the fleshy roots go deeper on their own where they will need no protection.

As a potted plant the taller varieties may need stakes. Put the stake in when you plant it, to avoid injuring the root. Allow the potted plant to die back in a cool—but not freezing—place before bringing it inside for the winter. Divide the roots only when the bloom is deteriorating, while the plant is dormant, or at the beginning of a new season of bloom. Wash the roots with a garden hose before dividing to allow you to see the roots clearly and to help you judge where to break them.

Uses: Cutting, wild garden, potted plant.

Amaryllis; see **_Hippeastrum_**

Amaryllis (am-a-RIL-is) **belladonna lily, naked lady, H,** easy, SU. ◑ ○ 🌢 🐝
Zones: 6 to 10
Height: 2 feet
Colors: Purplish pink, pink, white, rosy red, mauve (all colors usually with yellow throats)
Characteristics: Amaryllis is one of the most confusing names in the plant world. It is the Latin family name for a group of South African species, but is used also as the common name for a group of South American plants with the Latin family name of *Hippeastrum*.

The belladonna lily resembles members of the *Hippeastrum* family, and this adds to the confusion. However, the belladonna lily has solid stems, fat, rounded seeds and leaves that develop in late summer after the flowers have finished blooming. The *Hippeastrum* family has hollow stems and flat seeds, and the leaves are present while the flowers bloom.

The flowers of *A. Belladonna* are lilylike, each up to 3 inches in diameter. Its strap-shaped leaves are 18 inches to 2 feet long. They appear in spring and then die back before the clusters of 6 to 12 fragrant blossoms crown the 2-foot, naked stalks in late summer. Group it in perennial borders and plant it under baby's breath (*Gypsophila*) so it can bloom in a froth of tiny white blossoms. In Zones 9 and 10 it is as prolific as a weed. In warm climates it should be used like the lily in the summer garden border, planted close to full-leafed perennials to help hide its naked bottom. In any climate it is delightful planted in a pot for terraces and balconies.

Cultural Information: The belladonna lily has an egg-shaped bulb, 2 to 4 inches in diameter. It has been grown in Zone 6 and wintered over outdoors with the protection of a wall, southern exposure and a heavy winter mulch of salt hay. A slow-release fertilizer with very low nitrogen content is best. Plant the bulbs 4 to 6 inches deep in a well-drained location and don't disturb the roots unless necessary for division. Prepare and enrich the soil with compost, 9 inches to a foot below where the bulbs are to be placed. This will provide nourishment for the many years the bulbs will live. Plant 1 to 2 inches deep in Zones 9 and 10 but 6 to 9 inches deep in full sun in Zones 6 to 8.

For planting in pots, belladonna lily is more attractive when several bulbs are grouped in large containers. Leave the top half of the bulbs exposed

Amaryllis Belladonna

above the soil. Plant in a mix of equal parts peat moss, potting soil and builder's sand or perlite. Add a sprinkling of

Anemone blanda

Anemone nemerosa

Anemone Pulsatilla

ground limestone, following the directions on the package, to help keep the soil neutral. Keep the pot barely moist until foliage appears; thereafter, treat the plant as any other potted plant, watering regularly and fertilizing monthly. (It shouldn't be fertilized until the second summer, when its soil is depleted of nutrients. Then, when the plant starts to grow in early summer, a weak solution of a liquid fertilizer should be given regularly through the season.) When the leaves die down, keep the plant dry for a month and then give it a thorough soaking and keep it damp until the flower stalks appear. Winter the plant in its container in a frost-free location with light, withholding water; this will allow it to go dormant. It need not be repotted for several years; remove it from its pot only to propagate from the new bulbs that form around the base of the bulb. All parts of the plant are poisonous.

Uses: Potted plant, middle to the back of a border, naturalizing.

Amaryllis, hardy; see **Lycoris**

Anemone (a-NEM-o-nee) **windflower, lily of the field, poppyflowered anemone, Greek anemone, pasque flower, H,** easy, SP. ◐ ○ ✤

Zones: 6 to 9

Height: 6 to 16 inches

Colors: Red, purple, blue, white, pink, rose

Characteristics: Both hardy and tender herbaceous perennials belong to this genus. *Anemone blanda,* the windflower, is covered with masses of starry, daisy-like flowers and blooms longer than any other spring bulb when grown in partial shade and a rich soil. Windflowers come in white, pink and blue flowers, 2 inches across. Their blossoms open in sunlight and close at night and in cloudy weather, perhaps as protection from the pelting spring rains. The leaves are deeply lobed and make an attractive, ferny foliage (not unlike parsley). Blooms arrive in early March and last a month or more. They are a lovely sight as they naturalize, spreading freely in drifts woven together with a jumble of brilliant, dazzling color under deciduous trees (not yet leafed-out) and shrubs. This is a flower that needs to be planted by the dozens to be showy and arresting in the garden. It is wonderful lining a path or used as a groundcover for taller bulbs or perennials that bloom at the same time; try hybrid tulips, Virginia bluebells and columbine (*Aquilegia*).

The tender florist's anemone, *A. coronaria,* is long stemmed, with ruffs of two or three leaves just under the poppylike flower. In winter it can be grown as a potted plant, blooming in a sunny location under cool conditions— a cool greenhouse or sunroom is ideal.

A. nemorosa grows from 6 inches to a foot high and is also long blooming. It has smaller leaves than *A. blanda* and cup-shaped, drooping flowers in the softer colors of pink, purple and white. This is a favorite of mine.

A. Pulsatilla, the pasque flower, is an early spring-blooming flower, with cupped blooms of lavender filled with spun gold. It blooms in a silver mist of ferny foliage. "Blooms in fur coats," is how my youngest daughter describes *A. Pulsatilla*, noting the furry stems and underside of the petals. I doubt its "fur coat" helps keep it warm, but it does have a knack for surviving late-winter storms and cold whipping winds by closing its flowers and snuggling close to the earth. After its long bloom, windflower continues to be decorative in the garden with fluffy, feathery, gray seed heads that ride the winds to new, sometimes unpromising, sites where it grows nestled between the rocks.

Cultural Information: Some anemones have tuberous roots and some have rhizomes. In the Pacific Northwest, rhizomes multiply so rapidly they must be lifted and divided every year. It likes humus-rich, sandy, moist and well-drained soil, deeply prepared. *A. blanda* grows from tubers, resembling small black pieces of coal. You can't tell which side to plant up but it doesn't matter, the tuber will grow whichever way it is planted. Soak the tubers for 24 hours in tepid water before planting, except in the moist climates of the Pacific Northwest where soaking is unnecessary. Plant the tubers and rhizomes 2 to 4 inches apart and 3 inches deep. Plant in late October to late November to keep the foliage from growing in the warm autumn weather only to be struck down by killing winter frosts.

A. coronaria may be planted outdoors in fall or spring in mild or moderate climates. In cold climates, spring planting only is recommended, because tubers are not reliably hardy where winters are severe. For best results, start in a well-protected cold frame or indoors in a greenhouse or sunporch in late winter. After danger of heavy frost, move the started tubers to the garden for May and June bloom.

Tubers can be planted directly into the garden without a cold frame or indoor headstart. Select a warm, sheltered location under a deciduous tree, so that the plant receives sun during the period of its spring bloom and shade in summer. Don't let it get too dry. Rich, well-drained soil and ample moisture bring best results. Set the bulbs about 3 inches deep and space them 6 inches apart.

In moderate climates, mulch the soil well after the ground freezes in fall. In cold climates, dig up the tubers and let them dry for a few days. Store them in a dry, cool location until ready to replant in spring.

To grow in pots, plant 6 to 8 tubers 1 to 2 inches deep in a 6-inch-deep pot, using a good potting soil. Put the pot in a cool, dark place for several weeks to allow time for good root growth. Later, transfer the pot to a sunny windowsill; supply plenty of air circulation and water, and keep at about 65°F. When the anemones have finished blooming, withhold water and place the pot on its side (so you're not tempted to water it) in a dry, frost-free cellar; the foliage will die off and the tubers will become dormant. Store the tubers at 50° to 60°F in pots until ready to repot with a fresh potting mix in the spring.

Uses: Edging, naturalizing, bedding, groundcover.

Autumn crocus; see ***Colchicum***

Avalanche lily; see ***Erythronium***

Belamcanda (bel-am-CAN-da) **blackberry lily, H,** easy, SU. ○ ◑ ✿

Zones: 5 to 10
Height: 2½ to 3 feet
Color: Red with orange spots
Characteristics: Blackberry lily is a member of the iris family from India, where its tuberous roots are used as an antidote for the bites from the cobra snake. Like daylily flowers, the showy, red-spotted, orange flowers last only a day, but each tuber sends up many flower stalks and each stalk holds clusters of flowers. The many buds guarantee several weeks of continuous bloom in midsummer. In fall, the decorative seedpods split open and display seeds that resemble blackberries. The pods are often used for winter arrangements.

Cultural Information: The blackberry lily's tuberous roots can be planted in the spring or fall, 6 inches apart and covered with 1 inch of soil. The soil should be enhanced with compost and prepared to a depth of 9 inches below the tuberous roots to permit good drainage and to provide the plants with nutrition. In Zones 5 and 6 it is best to protect the roots with a winter mulch. The roots can be divided in spring or fall or the seed planted to produce flowering plants two years later.

Uses: Middle of a border, dried ornamental seedpods, woodland walk.

Belladonna lily; see ***Amaryllis***

Belamcanda species

Blackberry lily; see ***Belamcanda***

Bletilla (blet-ILL-a) **hardy orchid, H,** slightly challenging, SU. ◐ ❗ ✿
Zones: 5 to 9
Height: 12 to 15 inches
Colors: Purple to pink
Characteristics: The flowers of the hardy orchid *B. striata* resemble those of tender orchids with their five loose petals surrounding a bottom tubular petal. The flowers are lavender-pink with dark stripes 1 inch across inside the throat. There are six to eight flowers on a stem. They bloom in early summer for six weeks. The foliage is green and narrow, 10 to 12 inches long, with prominent lengthwise creases. Hardy orchid also grows well as a potted plant in northern zones, handy because the plant can be moved to ideal conditions.
Cultural Information: Soil should be well drained, rich and moist, one part topsoil, and one part leaf mold or peat moss. Plant the roots 6 inches apart and 4 inches deep. It's important that the ground be kept moist during the growing period. To induce dormancy, dig up the bulbs before fall frost and move any potted plants into a cool (above freezing) area for winter. Divide the clumps, the swollen underground stems that resemble tubers, in fall or spring.
Uses: Cutting, potted plant.

Blue lily of the Nile; see ***Agapanthus***

Blue puschkinia; see ***Puschkinia***

Bletilla

Caladium 'Candidum'

Caladium (ka-LAY-dee-um) **fancy-leafed caladium, T,** easy, SU, F. ◐ ○
Zones: 8 to 10
Height: 1 to 5 feet
Color: Deep green foliage intricately patterned with green, white, pink and red
Characteristics: Caladium, from the riverbanks of the Amazon, is grown for its very attractive and colorful leaves. It is one of the most popular foliage plants in shady or semishady areas, and is also suitable for growing indoors. Their gorgeous leaves come in variegated, colorful patterns, some garish, some simple and subtle, to add drama to gardens, pots and planters. *Caladium × hortulanum* has spear-shaped leaves, 6 to 24 inches long. It blooms outdoors from June to frost and thrives in hot, humid weather.

'Candidum', one of the more simply patterned—white leaves with green ribs and veins—is the most popular caladium for summer gardens. 'Pink Beauty' is garish with dark green leaves, red veins and pink splashes, but it is 'Freida Hemple' that takes the prize for brightness with its hot pink splashes and scarlet ribs, highlighted by a dark green border. I once planted a group of caladium in a woodland area where they couldn't be seen until the stroller rounded the corner. The look of surprise on the faces of the guests, greeted by such bright color in a quiet woodland setting, created quite a stir. Reactions range from love at first sight to loathing; few plants are so controversial.
Cultural Information: Caladium prefers very rich, damp but well-drained soil. Be careful not to allow the soil to dry out, as it requires plenty of water during the growing season. When the foliage flops over, gradually reduce water. Before first frost, dig up the tender tubers, leaving the soil that adheres to their roots, and dry them in an airy place away from sun for one week. Then remove dead foliage and excess soil and store them in dry peat moss or vermiculite over the winter at 55° to 60°F. Divide the tubers at planting time. Plant 1 inch deep and space 1 foot apart. In northern climates start the tubers indoors in flats filled with planting formula, then transplant them

Caladium *'Irene Dank'*

Caladium *'Galaxy'*

Camass; see *Camassia*

Camassia (ka-MAS-ee-a) **cam-ass, wild hyacinth, quamash, H,** Native American, easy, SP. ○ ◑ ❘ ✿

Zones: 3 to 10
Height: 1 to 4 feet
Colors: Creamy white, pale blue to lavender to dark violet
Characteristics: For centuries *Camassia* bulbs (*C. Quamash*) were a major source of food for the Nez Perce and other Indian tribes of the Pacific Northwest, people who fought bitterly for control of the moist meadows where *Camassia* was harvested. The bulbs are poisonous when eaten raw, but harmless and nourishing when cooked. Today *Camassia* is a popular plant in Europe and its stately beauty is all but neglected in its North American homeland. The spikes of starry blue flowers with slightly varying lengths of petals, seemingly arranged at random, are surrounded by dark green bracts and sparked with conspicuous yellow stamens. Their wonderful blue color complements every other flower. It is long blooming in late spring—a wonderful complement to late tulips

outside when day temperatures are consistently above 70°F. All parts of the plant are poisonous. *Forcing Instructions: C. × hortulanum* blooms indoors in winter and early spring. The tubers are grown indoors in the same way as begonia or gloxinia, except that caladium needs very warm (70° to 80°F) temperatures to start its growth. Plants will emerge from one to two weeks after planting. Use a 4-inch pot or pan with broken crockery or gravel over the drainage hole. Start in a good planting soil and then pot up in a soil more rich in humus. Good drainage is important. Plant just deep enough to cover the tubers, one per pot, and keep them well watered. Because it carries heavy leaves on skinny stems, the plant will need support as it grows.

A potted tuber that shows no signs of shoots after several weeks quickly comes to life when the container is set near a radiator or other source of heat, but be especially careful not to let the soil dry out. If the tuber is started in peat moss, make sure it is completely covered; roots do not develop well if the tuber is just set on top of the peat moss. Cut off any flowers that may develop, because they are not decorative and slow the plant's growth.
Uses: Potted plant, screen, background accent, bedding.

Camassia leichtlinii *'Blue Danube'*

and a wonderful source of unusual, arresting beauty. The flowers open from the bottom up and are beautiful in arrangements. *Camassia* quickly disappears when the blossoms have finished, so the plant doesn't distract from other garden attractions as the tulip and daffodil do. White varieties are available with flowers up to 4 feet tall, but I prefer the beautiful blue varieties, especially *C. leichtlinii* 'Blue Danube'.

Cultural Information: It adapts to many soils, even wet, poorly drained sites and clay. Plant *Camassia* in the fall, 4 inches deep and 6 to 8 inches apart. It is not a fussy plant. It expands slowly but surely, spreading iron roots through which nothing can grow in all directions. It is very showy when in bloom but leaves a blank spot in the garden when it has finished. Plant it near summer flowering, tough plants like daylilies, which will grow up to hide the soil the *Camassia* has left bare; don't plant fragile plants nearby as they will be crowded out over time.

Uses: Naturalizing (in woodlands and along streams and ponds), wild garden.

Canna *'Giant Mixed'*

Canna (KAN-a) **Indian shot, canna, T,** easy, SU. ○ ✿

Zones: 7 to 10

Height: 1½ to 6 feet

Colors: Many shades of yellow, red, pink, scarlet, white

Characteristics: Canna, which comes to us from Central and South America, is the boldest of bulbs with its height, husky structure and clusters of massive blooms in bright colors. Even from a distance, it is a show-stopper. Its tropical-looking leaves, green or bronze, remain attractive for a long time. Canna is best planted in large clumps of a single color where it can be enjoyed at a distance (it's good for park plantings). It is equally at home at the back of a border or in large tubs. The closely held flowers have been hybridized to include a generous range of color and color combinations in large and dwarf sizes. 'Wyoming', orange with bronze foliage, grows to 6 feet high. 'President' is glowing scarlet and stands 4 feet high. Dwarf Pfitzer canna is 2½ feet high and comes with such descriptive names as 'Chinese Coral', 'Primrose Yellow' and 'Salmon-Pink'. Dwarfs are an easier size to place in the home garden in front of shrubs, in a flower bed or in tubs on a patio.

Cultural Information: Canna thrives in sunny locations in fairly rich, moist, well-drained soil. For earlier bloom (especially in the North) start roots indoors about four weeks before danger of frost is past, transplanting outside when night temperatures stay above 50°F. Place the rhizomes 15 inches apart and 1 to 2 inches deep in a shallow box of light, sandy soil or peat moss. Water them well and keep them in a fairly warm, semidark place. Move the planting gradually into stronger light as the plants grow. They can be either potted up or left in the box until outdoor planting time.

When the weather is warm and settled set out the plants or roots 1½ to 2 feet apart and 3 to 4 inches deep. Keep the weeds from growing around them and supply ample moisture. Canna is a heavy feeder and likes to be "side dressed" (sprinkle fertilizer around—but not touching—the stem) with a complete, slow-release fertilizer.

When frost has blackened the foliage, cut the stalks off several inches above the ground and carefully dig up the clumps. Let them dry for a few days, then store in a cool, frost-free place at about 50°F. Pack the clumps in dry peat moss, sand, perlite or soil. Look them over occasionally, and if the roots show signs of withering, moisten slightly, but not enough to start growth. In the spring before planting, divide the roots, making sure that each division has several eyes. They need to be dug and reset in prepared soil only every three years.

Uses: Back of a border, tubs.

Checkered lily; see *Fritillaria*

Chionodoxa gigantea

Clivia *species*

Chionodoxa (ky-on-o-DOK-sa)
glory-of-the-snow, H, easy, W, SP. ○ ◑ ✿

Zones: 3 to 10

Height: 4 to 5 inches

Colors: Bright blue, light pink

Characteristics: Chionodoxa blooms in March, waving goodbye to the snowdrops, staying on to greet the daffodils. Glory-of-the-snow (*C. Luciliae*) has heavenly blue flowers with white-starred faces, the star sapphire of the garden. These jewels almost twinkle on a frosty, snowy day with 8 to 10 blossoms in a cluster, facing upward when blooming. The foliage is light green and unobtrusive, disappearing quickly after the flowers bloom. *C. Luciliae* 'Pink Giant' is a handsome pink variety. Plant in large colonies under deciduous trees or such groundcovers as rock cress (*Arabis*). If planting in beds, take care not to dig it up when planting in spring. These are very inexpensive bulbs and the first and the brightest blue of the season.

Cultural Information: Average, well-drained soil is all glory-of-the-snow asks for, but I have seen them growing beautifully on a hillside of heavy clay soil. Plant 1 to 3 inches apart and cover with 3 inches of soil. It requires normal moisture during the growing season, is undemanding and, planted where it can be left undisturbed, will increase rapidly, delighting you with its bright, cheery color year after year.

Uses: Edging, naturalizing, rock garden, companion plant.

Climbing lily; see *Gloriosa*

Clivia (KLY-vee-a) **kafir lily, T,** easy. ◑ 🐢 ✿

Zones: 9 and 10

Height: 12 to 15 inches

Colors: Orange to scarlet, with yellow throats

Characteristics: This native of South Africa can be grown as a winter-blooming houseplant. Each stem has globes of 12 to 20 fragrant, long-lasting flowers up to 3 inches wide. The straplike evergreen leaves, 18 to 24 inches long, gracefully arch over the edge of pots. The leaves stay attractive year 'round and don't die back. Water year 'round but fertilize only when it is time to bring *Clivia* into bloom.

Cultural Information: Clivia loves to have its crowded roots barely covered with soil; it shows its appreciation by blooming more. If planting in the garden, space 18 to 24 inches apart. If growing as a houseplant, use a good soil mix and give it bright, but indirect, sunlight. Cool night temperatures of 50° to 55°F and warmer day temperatures of 68° to 72°F will keep the plant in bloom longer. It can be propagated from the small secondary bulbs that form around the base of the planted bulb.

Uses: Potted plant, houseplant, frost-free border.

Colchicum (KOLE-chi-kum)
autumn crocus, H, easy, F. ○ ◑ ✿

Zones: 4 to 8

Height: 6 to 12 inches

Colors: Rosy purple, lilac

Characteristics: This large, cro-cuslike flower is a valuable addition to the fall garden. Originally from Asia Minor, it is as simple to grow as the daffodil and just as showy. It is easy to confuse the autumn-flowering crocus, a member of the iris family, with the colchicums,

Colchicum 'Lilac Wonder'

from the lily family, because it has similarly shaped and colored flowers. To be sure, count the number of stamens, the pollen-bearing, male organs in the center of the flower. The autumn-flowering crocus has three stamens and the colchicum has six stamens.

In spring, its leaves shoot up 15 inches and are tongue shaped. It is a beautiful green for a time, then turns a ghastly shade of yellow, appearing to be in agony and die back to the ground. Autumn-flowering crocus, on the other hand, sends up short, grasslike leaves in spring. The flowers, naked of any leaves, appear in fall. There is no sign from the plant from when the leaves die back in June until early fall, when naked stems 6 to 12 inches tall appear with flowers on top. Some of the larger flowers are top-heavy, but the stems are short so they rest on the ground. Plant colchicum under a groundcover of hosta, pachysandra, vinca, *Arabis*, *Iberis* or *Phlox subulata* for an attractive background when the plant flowers. It also helps to camouflage the ripening foliage. The corms are so independent they can even flower on a table, without water or soil and, if planted immediately after blooming, they will recover and bloom the next year.

The three most popular hybrid varieties all derive from *Colchicum autumnale*. 'Lilac Wonder' from Europe and North Africa, with vase-shaped, rosy purple flowers, is a prolific producer of blooms, up to 12 per corm. 'The Giant' has large goblets of lilac-pink flowers with white bases. 'Waterlily' resembles

its name, and blooms later with large, double, rosy lilac blooms (see page 24 for photo); it can produce as many as 6 flowers per corm. The corms are poisonous and can be planted without worry that they will be eaten by animals.

Cultural Information: Colchicum is best planted in late summer and will bloom in the garden in a few weeks. If planted later in the fall, it may have already flowered in its package but will still grow and flower normally the following autumn. Plant 4 to 6 inches deep and 8 inches apart in well-drained soil. Propagate it when its foliage has yellowed and died by digging up the large corms and removing the little corms that have developed around them. Replant both the large and small corms immediately.

Uses: Naturalizing, in the lawn, under a groundcover.

Convallaria (kon-val-AIR-ee-a) **lily of the valley, H,** Native American, easy, SP. ● ◐ ○ ⚱ 🌡 🦋

Zones: 3 to 9
Height: 5 to 8 inches
Colors: White, pink
Characteristics: The delightful fragrance of the lily of the valley announces itself the moment you enter the garden. The fragrance is so popular it is made available in soap, bubble bath, perfume and countless household products (including scented tissues). I prefer the real thing. *Convallaria majalis* is the most common variety grown, with five to eight white, drooping bells on each stem. The oval, green

leaves protectively wrap around the base of the plant and up the stem, allowing us only a glimpse of the white bells. To pick it for fragrance in the house, reach down into the leaves to cut enough of the stem to show its graceful arcing shape when arranged in a vase. It blooms in April and frequently continues as long as into June.

Lily of the valley is native to Europe, Asia and eastern North America. Orange berries follow the flowers but they are sparse and not very ornamental. The plant increases readily, making a good groundcover for shady locations—few plants can stand as much shade as it can. It is best planted where it can carpet the area. Weaker perennials could have a tough fight for space. In fall the leaves become ragged and unattractive when they yellow and die back to the ground, sometimes even before frost; don't remove them until they are absolutely dead. Once established the plant needs little attention. 'Rosea' has light pink flowers but is not as prolific a bloomer as the white varieties.

Cultural Information: An undemanding plant, lily of the valley will grow even in poor soils but not with the full, beautiful show it parades in well-prepared woodsy soils. It is not a true bulb but rather a spreading root from which pips, or single-growth buds with roots attached, sprout. Space the clumps of pips 4 to 6 inches apart and cover with 1 inch of soil.

Unlike many spring-blooming bulbs, lily of the valley stays green all summer and dies back in fall. For vigorous growth and

Convallaria majalis

abundant flowers, mulch lightly in the fall with compost or well-rotted cow manure, to supply nourishment for the coming spring. If the plant is all foliage, with no blooms, loosen and replenish the soil with compost before replanting the pips. The roots can be divided; make sure that each new root has its own pip. This can be done spring, fall or late summer.

Forcing Instructions: Lily of the valley can be forced into bloom from October to April. It emerges three weeks after planting. If the crowns have been kept dormant in cold storage at 28°F for three months or longer, they can be quickly forced into bloom. Plant them in a pot or bowl 5 to 6 inches deep, depending on the size of the clump. Set them in pebbles partially covered with water, or surround them with damp sphagnum moss. No soil is necessary, but they will have to be discarded after blooming. Plant the roots horizontally 1 inch deep with the pips just showing.

Uses: Cutting, rock garden, forcing.

Corn flag; see *Gladiolus*

Crocosmia (kro-KOZ-mee-a) **montbretia, H,** easy, SU. ○ 🌡 ❀

Zones: 6 to 10
Height: 2 to 3 feet
Colors: Gaudy orange, red, yellow
Characteristics: Crocosmia is a cousin of the gladiola from South Africa but is perfectly at home in northern climates with freezing and thawing weather. In mild climates it spreads rapidly and naturalizes. The plant has

six-petaled, star-shaped flowers in the brightest hues of yellow, orange and red. It blooms from the bottom to the top of the stem, opening on alternate sides. It creates bright spots in a mixed border and is well suited to pots and containers. *Crocosmia* 'Emily McKenzie' has bright orange flowers, with a circle of chocolate brown in the center of each, and *C.* 'Citronella' is covered with lemon yellow flowers.

Cultural Information: Plant the bulbs in the fall 6 inches apart in light, well-drained soil. Protect the bulbs during the first few years with a layer of dead leaves; once established they will no longer need the winter protection. Plant in bold groups of 10 or 12, rather than scattering them around the garden where they will be distracting.

Uses: Cutting, middle of a border.

Crocus (KRO-kus) **snow crocus, spring crocus, H,** easy, W, SP. ○ ◑ 🐞

Zones: 3 to 8
Height: 3 to 6 inches
Colors: Striped, bicolors, blushed or plain in various shades of white, yellow, pink, orange, red, purple
Characteristics: A harbinger of a new season, this early-blooming bulb announces that spring is indeed just around the corner. Starting with the colorful, cheery snow crocus and continuing with the larger, showier Dutch hybrids, *Crocus* provides a welcome display for weeks. And don't forget to look for the autumn-blooming crocus come October. Autumn-blooming crocus (*C. speciosus*) is a daintier species with a soft violet-blue flower, with darker veining than its

spring-blooming cousins. The long, elegant flowers appear before the leaves fall in early autumn and increase rapidly. It always catches me by surprise, looking a little out of place blooming in fall. However, it is very welcome when so many flowers have taken their leave.

All crocus increase quickly, bringing years of pleasure and, in some cases, a mild fragrance. The flowers are 1 to 2 inches

Crocosmia *'Citronella'*

Crocus speciosus, *fall-blooming crocus with hosta*

Crocus *'Snowstorm'*

Crocus *'Golden Bunch'—one of the earliest crocus to bloom*

long, wineglass shaped, on stems from 3 to 6 inches tall. It blooms from February through April and lasts for about two to three weeks. It makes the most dramatic appearance when planted in clumps of one color and is grown in with groundcovers.

The early species, the snow crocus, can be seen poking its little cups up through the snow. This bulb provides the first real flush of spring color. In the South it blooms in late January; it blooms in February or March in the North. It is noteworthy for its unusual color blends, not found in the larger hybrids. Even though it is only 3 to 4 inches tall it blooms so profusely that it is easily seen from a distance. 'Ruby Giant' (*C. Tomasinianus*) is especially dependable and long lived, among the best for naturalizing.

Dutch hybrid crocus, the large-flowered crocus, blooms just after the snow crocus and is a familiar and reassuring sight in early spring. Its cups of vivid, jewellike color make a welcome splash near an entryway, along walks, in a rock garden or at

Cyclamen neapolitanum

the front of a border. It can be naturalized in *Vinca minor* or ivy, but clumps of it are also lovely with early species of tulip or daffodil. 'Pickwick' is unusual for its lilac color with dark stripes. The Dutch hybrid 'Snowstorm', if planted in large quantities, would resemble pure white snow if not for the sparkling golden yellow stamens.

Saffron, used in cooking and also as a yellow dye, comes from the fall-blooming *C. sativus*. There are production farms in Spain where 7,000 to 8,000 crocus flowers are grown to produce 3½ ounces of saffron, which is why it is so expensive. The reddish lilac flowers open wide and the branched, flaming yellow pistil (the female part of the flower) is displayed. It is the end of the pistil, the stigma, that is dried for saffron.
Cultural Information: Crocus prefers an average to rich, well-drained soil. Plant it 1 inch deep in a lawn, but 2 to 4 inches deep in a garden bed, and space it 3 to 5 inches apart. It needs moisture to get its roots established after a fall planting. Over time, it multiplies prolifically. Dig the corms to divide or leave them until the plants lack bloom. Sometimes the corms work their way up to the surface and need to be replanted.
Forcing Instructions: Crocus can be forced to bloom anytime from December to April. The plant emerges eight weeks after planting at a temperature of 35° to 45°F. Use a 5-inch pot with good drainage material at the bottom such as broken pottery or a shallow layer of gravel or pebbles. (If the pebbles are small, place a small piece of screen over the

drainage hole to keep them from falling through.) The plant needs support, which is why the crocus bowls that provide holes for the flowers to grow through are popular. Half-fill the pot with a good planting formula. Plant the corms with their tops just below the rim of the pot and add soil until only the tips are visible. Plant them at a depth of 2 to 2½ inches. A 5-inch pot will hold 8 to 10 corms, spaced ½ inch apart. Water thoroughly either from the top or by immersing the entire pot in a tub of water and letting the excess water drain off. Follow the forcing directions on page 34.
Uses: Edging, naturalizing, rock garden, forcing.

Crocus, autumn; see *Colchium*

Crown imperial; see *Fritillaria*

Cyclamen (SIK-la-men or SY-kla-men) **hardy cyclamen, H,** moderate, F, W. ◐ ✽
Zones: 5 to 9
Height: 4 to 5 inches
Color: Lilac-pink
Characteristics: Hardy cyclamen (*C. neapolitanum*) looks like a miniature version of the cylamen that florists make available as potted plants during the holidays. It is amazing, blooming in the garden in October and November, waving its pastel, 1-inch flowers despite cold and nasty fall weather. Each bulb has 4 to 6 stems that will bloom over a six-week period. However, if left for many years, it could have hundreds of flowers. Its foliage is one of the wonders of nature. The heart-

shaped leaves are dark green marbled with silver, and remain green and beautiful throughout the winter, even under the snow. Sometimes the plant flowers again in late winter or early spring. It thrives under deciduous trees where, slowly but steadily, it increases in size. Roots grow from the top of the tuber as well as the bottom so be very careful when digging around them. The plant is so tiny it should be placed where it can be seen. I have it growing on top of a stone wall where you needn't bend over to look at it.

Cyclamen originated in Turkey. It's endangered because of uncontrolled collecting from the wild; the wild specimens are exported to Dutch nurseries where they are grown for a short time before being shipped to other countries. The plant is easily propagated and grown from seed. Before you buy, check to see that the nursery is growing its own, not endangering the plant's natural existence by importing it.
Cultural Information: The tubers must be planted concave side up, ½ inch deep, in rich soil and in a place protected from the harsh fall winds, rains and snow. The soil must be well drained but moist, as hardy cyclamen resents drying out. Don't plant anything on top of it. It is slow to multiply and prefers to be left undisturbed in a snug spot, under the outskirts of a shrub or next to a wall. Deep snow helps its survive and should not be removed.
Uses: Edging, rock garden, naturalizing.

Daffodil; see *Narcissus*

Dahlia; for information on *Dahlia,* see *Burpee American Gardening Series: Annuals*

Desert candle; see *Eremurus*

Dodecatheon (do-dek-ATH-eon) **shooting star, H,** Native American, difficult, SP. ◖

Zones: 4 to 10
Height: 18 inches
Colors: White, rose, lavender
Characteristics: The flowers of the shooting star rise on thin stems and have swept-back petals that give the appearance of flowers in flight. The broad, short leaves form flat rosettes at the base of the long stems and the flowers on top move easily with the gentle breezes. Shooting star blooms like a miniature fireworks display. It flowers for a few weeks in May or June. Shortly after flowering, the plant produces seed, withers and dies back to the ground where it is dormant until the following spring. After its short growth cycle of only three months, it is dormant. Because it is dormant nine months of the year, it is important to mark where the plant is so it is not accidently dug up or damaged. For this reason it is a plant for the dedicated or experienced gardener. It is native to the dry prairies and woodlands from the East Coast to the Midwest.
Cultural Information: Enrich the soil for shooting star with peat moss and leafmold. The soil must be rich in organic matter, able to hold enough water to feed the plant right through spring. Plant 8 inches apart in early fall or in March. An organic mulch of compost or shredded leaves keeps it moist during its

active period and, as it breaks down, provides nutrients for the next season's flowers. It produces bulblets the size of rice around its root at the time of flowering. Let the clumps fill out before dividing in spring or fall. The difficulty of dividing in the fall when the plant is invisible above ground makes spring division more reliable. Propagation is easier by seeds that are sown shortly after they are ripe. Sometimes, if happy, it will self-seed. (I had a clump appear 10 feet from its parent and grow in a rocky crevice.)
Uses: Woodland plantings, naturalizing, rock garden.

Dogtooth violet; see *Erythronium*

Endymion hispanicus (en-DEE-mion hi-SPAN-ikus) **wood hyacinth, Spanish squill, H,** easy, SP. ◖ ● ◗ ✿

Zones: 4 to 8
Height: 15 inches
Colors: White, blue, pink
Characteristics: The wood hyacinth (formerly called *Scilla campanulata* and *S. hispanica*) is among the latest spring bulbs to flower. It bears graceful, delicate, bell-like blooms on sturdy,

Dodecatheon *species*

Endymion hispanicus

Eremurus himalaicus

erect spikes, embellished by green, ribbonlike leaves from May to early June. Its pastel colors are a lovely complement to the vivid colors of tulips and azaleas. It is extremely easy to grow and seems to live forever, forming impressive colonies.
Cultural Information: Grow as for *Scilla.* Plant bulbs 3 to 4 inches deep and 6 to 8 inches apart.
Uses: Naturalizing, cutting, shady border.

Eranthis (e-RAN-this) **winter aconite, H,** moderate, **W.** ◖✿

Zones: 4 to 9
Height: 3 to 4 inches
Color: Yellow
Characteristics: A native of Europe and Asia, winter aconite is a member of the buttercup family (*Ranunculaceae*), and there is a distinct family resemblance. The yellow buttercuplike flowers of *E. hyemalis,* 1 inch across with green frilled collars, appear in late February or early March. In addition to the medium green, ruffled leaves that form the collar below the blossom, it has other foliage that is

Eranthis *species*

shaped like palm leaves. Winter aconite blooms in February and stays through March if the weather is to its liking. It may remain in bloom for almost two months. Its palm leaf foliage is attractive in the garden after the flowers fade.

Winter aconite is beautiful as a carpet under deciduous trees or planted under English ivy. It can be combined with some of its friends whose blooms overlap or blossom at the same time: species crocus, *Puschkinia,* snowdrops and glory-of-the-snow.
Cultural Information: Winter aconite bulbs dry up when kept out of the ground for any length of time—for this reason there is a significant casualty rate for mail-order purchases, as they frequently don't survive long enough to be put into the ground. Never store the bulbs, but plant immediately upon receipt. If you can't plant them when you receive them, store them in damp peat moss in a cool place. The best time to transplant them is when they are in flower. However, unless you have a very generous friend with a large planting of winter aconite, this is impossible because it is available from catalogs and nurseries only in fall.

Once it lives through the first winter, it is undemanding and multiplies freely in the garden. It prefers humus-rich soil and regular watering. Plant 2 to 3 inches deep and 3 to 4 inches apart. Heat will cause the flowers to wilt and will reduce the flowering period. It blooms in late winter but can withstand snow and sleet, blooming close to the ground where it has some protection. The attractive, finely

cut foliage lasts for several months, disappearing in mid-May. Mark the garden area where it is planted so bulbs are not disturbed. Its tuberous roots, once established, increase rapidly by both seed and division. Thriving in the cool shade of deciduous trees, it grows taller when given moist soil.
Uses: Naturalizing, rock garden.

Eremurus (er-e-MEW-rus) **foxtail lily, desert candle, king's spear, H,** Native American, moderate, SU. ○ 🌡

Zones: 5 to 9
Height: 2 to 9 feet
Colors: White, yellow, pink, orange-yellow
Characteristics: Foxtail lily grows to impressive height and produces showy, arresting flowers. It is hard to understand why it is so seldom grown in American gardens. Hundreds of small blossoms cover the tapering top of the stems, making it look indeed like a fluffy foxtail. It takes up very little room in the middle of a border, but should be planted where it is protected from strong winds. It is showiest when planted in front of an evergreen background, which sets off its colors.

It is a member of the lily family (*Liliaceae*) from temperate Asia and is native to the Himalayas. *Eremurus himalaicus* blooms in early summer with white flowers crowded together on 2- to 3-foot-tall stems. *E. Bungei,* from Iran and Russia, has clear yellow flowers that reach 4 feet tall. These varieties make good additions to the cutting garden.
Cultural Information: Eremus starts to grow early in spring. In northern zones it should be

protected with salt hay or pine boughs until all danger of frost is past. Once established, it is long-lived. It is best not to transplant but to leave it. It requires good drainage and nutritious soil. To ensure good drainage it can be set on an inch or two of sand. Its roots need to be handled gently as they grow out like spokes of a wheel and are brittle and easily broken. Plant them 6 inches deep and space a foot or more apart.

Uses: Middle of a border, cutting.

Erythronium (er-i-THRO-nee-um) **dogtooth violet, trout lily, adder's tongue, avalanche lily, fawn lily, star lily, H,** Native American, moderate, SP. ◐ ▮

Zones: 3 to 9
Height: 6 to 24 inches
Colors: Yellow, pink, cream, lavender, rose
Characteristics: You can see by its numerous nicknames that dogtooth violet is a plant that has been noticed and loved by gardeners across the country. There are 25 known species, most of them Native American plants. Little grown in gardens, it should be planted more frequently. It resembles a miniature lily and blooms in the spring, a time when the garden could use more flowers.

Erythronium Dens-canis is the lone European species, and arrived here with the settlers. Its nickname, "dogtooth violet," seems strange for so beautiful a flower, but its name is derived from the long white bulbs, which do look like fangs. Cultivation was first recorded in 1596. The delicately scented plant hugs the ground while the nodding, lily-like flowers rise above, flipping the tips of their petals back. Twin, bright green, exquisitely mottled leaves carpet the ground. Nature has given it a natural camouflage, as though filtered sunlight were reflecting brownish red shadows on it. It blooms in April and lasts two to three weeks. It likes to be planted at the base of trees or in a woodland setting. Generally it takes several years to become established.

E. × *hybrid* 'Pagoda' (a good description for the reflected—turned back—petals) is a hybrid garden variety with clusters of four or five nodding, butter yellow blossoms and marbled foliage that makes its appearance in April.

E. grandiflorum is taller, 24 inches high, and has golden yellow flowers, frequently streaked with green on the outside; its green leaves are plain, not mottled. *E. Hendersonii* is the pink trout lily from the West Coast, but it is perfectly reliable in eastern gardens. *E. revolutum* has been called the aristocrat of the clan for its quiet, stately beauty, boasting several flowers to a stem. The flowers open pale, almost white, and as they mature take on a delicate lilac blush.

Cultural Information: If you can't plant *Erythronium* when you receive it, keep it in slightly damp peat moss in a cool, shaded place. Plant with the thin end of the corms facing up, about 3 inches deep in moist soil, rich in humus, and give it the dappled shade of deciduous trees. It dislikes extreme heat and dryness. Keep it well watered (not waterlogged) until the plant is established. A mulch of shredded leaves, pine needles or compost will keep it moist. After the plant flowers, leave it undisturbed. Set the bulbs 2 or 3 inches apart, 3 inches deep; to make an effective showing, it needs a close planting. It propagates by self-seeding but the seeds take a year to germinate and three or four more to flower.

Uses: Naturalizing, rock garden, woodland garden.

Eucomis (YEW-ko-mis) **pineapple lily, T,** easy. ◑ ○ ▮ ✿

Zones: 9 and 10
Height: 2 to 3 feet
Colors: Purple spotted white, pink or wine
Characteristics: As its common name suggests, *Eucomis* resembles pineapples blooming atop tall stems. Tufts of green leaves crown cylindrical flower spikes covered in starry blossoms. The leaves emerge from the base of the stem and arch in a fountain shape; they resemble the leaves of the daylily, except with creases in the middle. *Eucomis* is summer blooming and is easily grown in pots or in the garden. It also makes unusual cut flowers. It is a member of the lily family from South Africa.

Cultural Information: Plant pineapple lilies 6 inches apart and 3 to 4 inches deep in a rich soil with good drainage. It can remain undisturbed for many years in pots or in the garden. Transplant after the foliage dies back or in the early fall. It likes moist soil while growing, but needs a dryer soil when dormant.

If growing in a pot, plant one per 5-inch pot or three together in a larger pot. The pots should be brought in before fall frost

Erythronium *'Pagoda'*

Eucomis *species*

Freesia 'Single Mixed Colors'

Fritillaria Meleagris

and given a rest and protection in a place where the temperature stays cool but above 40°F. *Uses:* Potted plant, middle of a border.

Fancy-leafed caladium; see *Caladium*

Fawn lily; see *Erythronium*

Flowering onion; see *Allium*

Foxtail lily; see *Eremurus*

Freesia (FREE-zha) **freesia, T,** easy. ○ ▮ ✿ ❀
Zones: 9 to 10
Height: 12 to 18 inches
Colors: Yellow, white, pink, scarlet, lavender, copper
Characteristics: Freesia is well known for its sweet fragrance, pronounced but never overpowering. Its graceful form, flexible stems and wide range of clear, bright colors are attributes that make it an ideal cutting flower. (This is perhaps how it is best known, readily available from florists.) However, it is an easy, winter-flowering plant for the home gardener to grow indoors too.

Tecolote hybrids, grown in California, are more compact with strong stems, particularly suited to pot culture. Each funnel-shaped bloom is either single or double and hangs on loose spikes. Foliage is long, narrow, medium green leaves. The plant lacks backbone and becomes quite floppy—it nearly always needs staking. Originally from South Africa, it is a member of the iris family (*Iridaceae*).
Cultural Information: Except in frost-free areas of the country, freesia is grown indoors at

moderately low temperatures for winter and spring flowering. Flowers appear about three months after the corms are planted. The soil should be rich and porous with good drainage. Plant the bulbs 3 inches deep and 3 inches apart. Keep the soil moist during the growing season, especially during dry spells. Remove dead flowers to extend the bloom. In fall, before the first frost, dig the corms and bring them inside. Keep them in a cool, dry place where they can remain dormant for a minimum of four months before they are repotted and stimulated with water and light to rebloom.
Forcing Instructions: Freesia doesn't need a cold period, but it does need a dormant period. Grow in a cool, sunny spot in winter. A cool greenhouse or sunroom is ideal. Plant the corms at two-week intervals from September to December to give a succession of bloom. It blooms indoors from winter into early spring and each bulb continues flowering for about 6 weeks. The plant emerges 2 to 3 weeks after planting and comes into bloom in 12 weeks at a temperature of 40° to 50°F. Use a 6-inch pot with good drainage material such as pebbles or a gravel layer in the bottom; it will hold a dozen corms. The top of each corm should be planted just below the soil's surface, and the soil kept moist. When the top growth is 1 to 2 inches high, move to a sunny, cool window with a temperature of approximately 55°F. Keep the soil moist and fertilize with a liquid fertilizer solution every 10 days from the time the flower buds appear. Support the stems with stakes to

prevent them from bending under the weight of the flowers. Too much water at first and too-high temperatures may inhibit bloom.

After the flowers have faded and the foliage turns yellow, remove the stems close to the base. Put the pots in a cool place and gradually withhold water. The soil should be dry and the bulbs dormant for about four months. When growing for cutting flowers don't cut the foliage, only the flowers, if you want to reuse the bulbs the next year. When keeping bulbs from year to year, it is important to build up their strength with fertilizer and to keep their soil moist until the leaves yellow and die. The bulbs can be stored in their pots but they must be repotted before they are brought into bloom again.
Uses: Forcing, potted plant, cutting, frost-free garden.

Fritillaria (fri-ti-LAIR-ee-a) **crown imperial, checkered lily, guinea-hen lily, H,** moderate, SP. ◑ ○ ▮
Zones: 3 to 9
Height: 6 to 36 inches
Colors: Yellow, orange, red, purple, bicolors of white and purple
Characteristics: Gardeners have dubbed *Fritillaria* "the problem child of the lily family." It isn't that it is difficult. It simply expects its perfectly reasonable requests to be granted, and we're not always sure what those requests are. The genus *Fritillaria* is a curious and strange group, including more than 85 species, only a handful of which are available to gardeners. It is native to northern, temperate, mountainous regions from Iran

Fritillaria imperialis

Galanthus nivalis

are), whereas other varieties are smooth.

F. Meleagris differs from other *Fritillaria* and most spring bulbs in that it prefers a moist soil that must not dry out during hot weather. It can also be divided after its foliage dies. Dig, separate and replant it immediately. *Fritillaria* will not be bothered by rodents.

Uses: Naturalizing, edging, bedding, companion plant, rock garden, containers.

Galanthus (ga-LAN-thus)
snowdrop, H, easy, W. ○ ◑ 🌡️ 🌸 ❁

Zones: 3 to 9
Height: 3 to 4 inches
Color: White
Characteristics: The first of the faithful little bulbs cheerfully announcing spring, snowdrop returns fearlessly to the garden year after year undeterred by onslaughts of snow and ice. It can be planted and forgotten. It has a sweet, subtle fragrance that perfumes the air when it is grown in large, naturalized colonies. Bring a small clump inside where warm air will spread the fragrance throughout the room. Its flowers of nodding bells are 1 inch long and white, blooming above slender, long, green foliage. It blooms in January and February into March and last three weeks or longer. The bulbs in my garden were planted more than 80 years ago and they continue to increase and bloom in little clumps with their frosted bells almost touching. I have never divided them and they have never diminished in bloom.

The easiest to naturalize is the common snowdrop, *Galanthus*

to India. Most species have drooping or nodding flowers and are low growing. The crown imperial (*F. imperialis*) is a stately (3- to 4-foot), beautiful spring flower. Standing tall, it presides over the kingdom of smaller spring bulbs. A circle of large, drooping, bell-shaped, yellow, reddish or burnt orange flowers each 1½ inches long, is crowned by a 2-inch tuft of green leaves. Three crown imperials planted among two dozen daffodils is very showy.

The crown imperial has a slightly pungent (some people call it skunky), scent, but unless you bend to take a whiff you probably will not notice it. It blooms in late April for about two weeks. 'Rubra Maxima', with red flowers, 'Lutea Maxima', with yellow flowers and 'Aurora', with orange flowers, are superior varieties. *F. Meleagris*, the checkered lily or guineahen lily, is nature's checkerboard, superbly mottled with a fascinating design in muted shades of bronze, purple and white, all checkered, striped or splashed with contrasting colors. The foliage is light green and graceful, similar to the leaves of lilies.

F. pudica is an American native, but hard to find. *F. biblora* is the 18-inch-tall, black or chocolate lily of southern California. Also recommended are *F. persica* 'Adiyaman', dramatic 30-inch spikes with bell-shaped, almost black flowers and good for forcing, and *F. Meleagris* 'Chailovskyi', 4 to 10 inches, with 1-inch bells of chocolate purple tipped with yellow.

Cultural Information: *Fritillaria* likes sweet (alkaline) soils of deep, sandy loam, very well drained and with plenty of compost for food. Remember to add lime if necessary. *F. imperialis* is planted 6 inches deep and 8 inches apart, while all other varieties should be 3 to 4 inches deep and 3 to 4 inches apart. It needs deep watering in the spring but prefers dry conditions in the summer while the bulb is dormant. Cut off the flowers and stalks after they bloom to prevent it from going to seed and to conserve energy for building next year's flowers. Once established, the plant should never be disturbed. Some varieties, like the crown imperial, are covered with thick, overlapping scales (as true lilies *nivalis*. There is a giant version, *G. Elwesii*, with slightly wider leaves and larger flowers, better behaved in the South but slow to naturalize in the North. *G. nivalis* 'Plenus' is a double-flowered snowdrop with crisp, white outer petals surrounding an inner rosette striped with light green. Because the snowdrop bows its head, the double flower can only be seen if you pick it or bend down and lift up its head.

Cultural Information: Snowdrop is an undemanding plant and any soil is good as long as it stays moist. Plant it 3 inches deep and 3 inches apart where it can be left undisturbed for years. Its leaves wither soon after the flowers die, so the plant is good for planting in the lawn. The best time to divide it is right after flowering.

Forcing Instructions: Use a 6-inch pot with good drainage material such as broken crockery, gravel or pebbles in the bottom, and cover with a good planting formula. Plant the bulbs ½ inch deep and space them 2 to 4 inches apart. Water them well and place them in a cool area to develop their roots for 8 to 10 weeks. Then bring them into a warm, light area. They will emerge several weeks later.

Uses: Edging, naturalizing, rock garden, forcing.

Galtonia species

Galtonia (gal-TOH-nee-a) **summer hyacinth, T,** easy, SU. ○ ❗ ❀ ✿

Zones: 8 to 10
Height: 3 to 4 feet
Color: White
Characteristics: Summer hyacinth blooms for a month in the summer with 20 to 30 bell-shaped fragrant flowers dangling from

Butterfly Gladiolus
'Mixed Colors'

tall stems. The strap-shaped long leaves are 2 to 3 feet long. Planted between plants of *Yucca filamentosa* to bloom after the *Yucca*, it makes for a handsome combination, and the plants and their roots are compatible. (The leaves and flowers of the two plants are the same shape and arch in the same way, but the *Galtonia* is considerably smaller than the *Yucca*.)

Cultural Information: Plant summer hyacinth bulbs 15 inches apart and 6 to 7 inches deep in a rich, well-drained soil. In Zones 5 to 7 it can be left in the garden, provided it is planted in a protected spot with southern exposure and heavily mulched with salt hay or pine boughs to keep the bulbs from freezing. Propagate the bulbs by removing the small bulbs that form around the mother bulb. In areas with frost summer hyacinth is treated like gladiola, dug and wintered indoors to be replanted the following summer.

Uses: Potted plant, middle to back of a border.

Giant allium; see *Allium*

Gladiola; see *Gladiolus*

Gladiolus (gla-dee-O-lus) **gladiola, sword lily, corn flag, T & H,** easy, SU. ○ ❗ ❀

Zones: 8 to 10
Height: 3 to 6 feet
Colors: Cream, blues, purples, pinks, yellows, reds
Characteristics: The gladiola's stately and formal appearance has led to its overuse in funeral arrangements and its unfortunate stereotype as the flower most associated with death. Consequently, it is overlooked

and undergrown in today's cutting gardens. The individual ruffled, plain or bicolored flowers range in size from 2½ to 5½ inches wide. The foliage is green and sword shaped. Blooms last from midsummer to frost. The flowers at the bottom of the stalk tend to die before the flowers at the top open, so if it is planted in a border it is better to plant it behind 2-foot-tall flowers that will hide the bottom of the gladiola.

The hardy gladiola (hardy to Zone 7) is similar to the more-familiar tender gladiola, except the flower spikes are shorter, looser and bear smaller flowers. The flowers are butterfly shaped in shades of rose, pink, white and some bicolors, with contrasting blotches. Flowers are widely spaced along 18- to 20-inch flower spikes, creating a vivid splash of color for several weeks when they bloom in early June. They are long lasting in bouquets.

Cultural Information: An adaptable flower, the gladiola does best in a sunny location protected from the wind. (An exposed location is satisfactory if the plants are staked.) Deeply prepared, rich or light, sandy loam is best, but almost any soil rich in compost, leaf mold or peat moss will do. It should be slightly acid to neutral, well worked and enriched with a slow-release fertilizer. Plantings can be made in spring as soon as the ground is in workable condition. If continuous display is desired, successive plantings may be made every two weeks until the first of July. Flowering time varies greatly, depending on the variety and the size of the corms as well as growing conditions. The average time for bloom is 75 to 90 days after planting. To avoid disease, it is recommended that the corms be soaked for an hour immediately before planting in a solution of 1½ tablespoons Lysol per gallon of water. The corms are then planted 4 to 6 inches deep and 6 to 8 inches apart. If planting in pots, plant them a few inches deeper and you might avoid having to stake. It needs an abundance of moisture during its growing period, and an organic mulch is important to help conserve moisture.

The care of gladiola consists of providing it with enough moisture through regular watering. The flower spikes should be removed after flowering, as the development of seedpods will decrease the size of the corms, affecting the next year's bloom. Cutting too much foliage with the flowers is detrimental. It is best to leave four to six leaves on the plant to help replenish the corm. Keep the corms growing until all the foliage turns brown. After the first killing frost, dig up the corms and spread them out to dry in an airy, frost-free place. After a few weeks shake off the soil, remove any remaining foliage, and divide the old (or "mother") corm from the small cormlets. Store the corms indoors over winter at around 40°F, in old nylon stockings or onion bags (so that air will circulate among them). The following spring, plant the cormlets in rows next to the mother bulbs. It will be two years before they bloom, but they will send up grasslike foliage, which is decorative the first year. The cormlets' foliage might be a month later

in appearing than the mother bulb because their outer casing is very hard; don't assume they are dead and dig them up too early.

Unlike corms of the summer-blooming gladiola, hardy gladiola corms are planted in the fall, 3 to 4 inches deep and spaced closer but at least 4 inches apart. Groups of a dozen or more corms create an attractive planting. Although hardy gladiola will grow in most soils, it seems to prefer light, sandy loam enriched with compost, leaf mold or peat moss. Avoid the use of manures as these tend to encourage bulb rot. Fertilize with a slow-release fertilizer, sprinkled on the ground after the bulbs are planted; repeat every fall thereafter. When it becomes obvious that your hardy gladiolas are overcrowded or are not blooming as they should, it is an indication the corms need to be separated and replanted—the sooner, the better.

Uses: Cutting, bedding.

Gloriosa (glor-ee-O-sa) **climbing lily, T,** slightly challenging. ○ ◑ ⬯ ❀

Zones: 8 to 10
Height: 4 to 6 feet
Colors: Red and yellow
Characteristics: Climbing lily can be grown outside as an annual vine or in the home or greenhouse as a potted plant. The flowers are striking combinations of red and yellow with reflexed, lilylike, curved stems—very showy in the garden, especially in full sun when the colors are more vivid and the plants fuller. The leaf tips elongate to curling tendrils that cling to a fence, trellis, string or wire. The plant may reach a height of 6 feet if

given support on which to climb. It is tender and should be planted after all danger of frost is past. It should be dug up in fall and wintered indoors, except in frost-free areas where the plant may be left in the ground year 'round. Outdoors the blooms last from summer through fall and make excellent cutting flowers.
Cultural Information: The climbing lily is unlike any of the other lilies. It does not have scales, and is somewhat like dahlia tubers, 4 to 6 inches long and a trifle thicker than a lead pencil. Tubers obtained before the proper planting time should be stored in a cool, dry, dark place and covered with dry soil, sand, peat moss or vermiculite. Be careful not to damage the pinkish bud shoots at one end of the tuber.

To plant directly outdoors, dig a hole at least 6 inches deep and work in plenty of sand, leaf mulch and/or peat moss. If the soil has a tendency to pack, extend the area being prepared and use more sand to increase the drainage. Set the tubers in a horizontal position 2 to 4 inches deep and 1 foot apart near a trellis or fence that the plants can climb. Cover and water thoroughly and regularly until the shoots appear. Afterward, keep the soil moist but not soggy. After flowering, when the plants yellow and the foliage dies down, dig the tubers up carefully. They may be several inches deeper than when originally planted, so dig carefully. Clean the tubers before dividing them or separating the smaller tubers that develop beside the large ones, and dust them with sulfur to prevent disease and

Gloriosa superba

Hippeastrum
'Apple Blossom'

Hippeastrum 'Red Lion'

rotting. Store the bulbs in dry peat moss at 55° to 60°F until the pink buds, or eyes, are formed; this takes approximately three months. They can be re-planted as before, giving two sets of bloom in one year. The smaller tubers are stored the same way as the larger tubers.
Forcing Instructions: If planting in pots, cover the tubers with 2 to 4 inches of soil, the larger ones deeper than the smaller ones, in a pot with drainage holes. Climbing lily likes very rich, well-drained soil, two parts rich potting soil, one part build-ers' sand and one part peat moss. If you want it to climb up, rather than sprawl down, put a trellis in the pot at the same time you plant the tubers to avoid damaging the roots that will develop later. Keep the soil evenly moist and leave in a fairly warm room (55° to 65°F) with indirect light until growth be-gins. Gradually bring the plant into the light and increase the water, keeping the soil moist at all times and not allowing the temperature to go above 65°F. After flowering is finished, with-hold water and fertilizer as the vine dies down, allowing the plant to go dormant. After bloom, lift and store as described above.
Uses: Cutting, potted plant, greenhouse plant, small corsage.

Glory-of-the-snow; see ***Chionodoxa***

Grape hyacinth; see ***Muscari***

Greek anemone; see ***Anemone***

Guinea-hen lily; see ***Fritillaria***

Hardy amaryllis; see ***Lycoris***

Hardy cyclamen; see ***Cyclamen***

Hardy orchid; see ***Bletilla***

Hippeastrum (hip-ee-AS-trum)
amaryllis, T, easy. ○ ◐ 🌡 ❀
Zones: 8 to 10
Height: 12 to 20 inches
Colors: White, pink, red, rose, salmon, some striped
Characteristics: Among the eas-iest and fastest growing of all indoor bulbs, amaryllis will de-light you with its big, bold, trumpet-shaped flowers. These appear on stems about 18 inches high, often before the foliage appears. The blooms are up to 8 inches across, usually pro-duced four to a stem, and each bulb, depending on its size, sends up one to three stems. For showy blossoms, buy bulbs that are between 26 and 30 cen-timeters or larger.

In frost-free areas of the South and West, amaryllis also makes a fine garden plant; it may be left untended year after year. In cooler areas it will rebloom in succeeding years if dormancy is provided for.

H. gracilis dulcinea 'Scarlet Baby' is an exciting new dwarf amaryllis whose compact form and free blooming make it a marvel for the outdoor garden. It generally grows no higher than 12 inches, topped with brilliant scarlet-red flowers. Although each bloom is smaller than those of the more familiar hybrids, each stalk may produce six or more of them, and each bulb can produce several stalks.

Some of the most popular am-aryllis include 'Apple Blossom'

with white, pink-striped blooms, 'Red Lion', a Christmas favor-ite for its velvety crimson pet-als and their glossy sheen and 'Prince Carnival' with rich red stripes on a white background.
Cultural Information: Amaryl-lis bulbs should be potted as soon as they are received. Use of two parts good potting soil to one part peat moss or perlite. Pots should be deep and about 1 inch wider than the bulb di-ameter. Amaryllis does well in average home temperatures of 65° to 75°F, although bloom will last longer and growth will be slower at 55° to 65°F. Water sparingly until flower bud and stem appear, giving more water as the stem elongates and even more during bloom. If too much water is given immediately af-ter planting, sometimes only fo-liage will be produced. Be sure there is ample drainage; never allow water to stand in the saucer. Applications of water-soluble houseplant food (according to the manufacturer's directions) will benefit growth and bloom. When the bulb has finished blooming, cut the flower stalk down to about 1 inch from the top of the bulb. Let the foliage continue to develop. Amaryllis blooms from three to eight weeks after planting in fall and win-ter. Rotate the pot when the plant is in flower to keep each stem growing straight. Bulbs can be left in the pots after flower-ing but you may need to add new soil to pots each year.

The pots may be buried up to their rims in a sheltered place to allow their foliage to ripen in the garden after danger of frost and when the nights have be-come warm. In fall, before frost, take up the pots or bulbs and place them in a dry, frost-free location. Let the foliage die down and keep the soil barely moist. As new growth appears, two to three months later, bring the pots gradually to the light to start the bulbs growing again. Repot only if the bulb becomes root-bound.

Uses: Edging, cutting, forcing, potted plant, greenhouse plant.

Hyacinth; see *Hyacinthus*

Hyacinth, grape; see *Muscari*

Hyacinth, summer; see *Galtonia*

Hyacinth, wild; see *Camassia*

Hyacinth, wood; see *Endymion*

Hyacinthus orientalis

(hy-a-SIN-thus) **hyacinth, H,** easy, SP. ○ ◑ ❚ ✿.
Zones: 5 to 10
Height: 10 inches
Colors: Pastel pink, pastel blue, salmon, white, yellow, purple; magenta and violet may have stripes along the petals' edges
Characteristics: Few spring flowers can rival the hyacinth for sweet fragrance.

More imposing and formal than that of other bulbs, hyacinth beauty has been exploited over the centuries with an inclination to formal bedding in circles, half-moons, crescents, stars and other artificial shapes cut into lawns. Hyacinth looks best planted in beds joined by other flowers where its short bloom period is supplemented by longer-flowering bulbs and

perennials. It looks outstanding in clumps in the foreground of a border, where perennials will grow up around it and hide its dying foliage. Standing only about 10 inches tall, hyacinth is one of the few bulbs planted to good effect in rows, as an edging, for example. I like it better growing in part shade because it appears looser and relaxed. Hyacinth blooms in April for two to three weeks. If you don't have a cutting garden, plant a few plants in the vegetable garden, so you can harvest them and bring them into the house to spread their wonderful fragrance.

Cultural Information: Hyacinth prefers full sun but it will tolerate part shade and can be planted under deciduous trees. It likes loam soil with good drainage. Keep it well watered, once a week if the season is dry. After the flower dies, cut off the flower stems and let the foliage dry up. Plant the bulbs 4 to 5 inches deep and between 4 and 8 inches apart.

The alternate freezing and thawing of northern winters is hard on all bulbs but the hyacinth seems to suffer the most. As the flowers get smaller, replace the bulbs every two to three years. It is especially helpful to protect them with mulch.

Forcing Instructions: Hyacinth usually blooms indoors in December through April or later. It emerges 8 weeks after planting at 35° to 45°F. Plant it in a 4- to 5-inch pot with good drainage material, broken crockery or pebbles, in a shallow layer in the bottom of the pot. The soil should be one part potting soil, one part coarse peat moss and one part builder's sand, with a sprinkling of ground limestone added according to the manufacturer's directions. No fertilizer is needed. Plant the bulbs with their tops just below the soil line—don't press them into the soil. Space the bulbs ½ inch apart and from the sides of the pot. Water thoroughly from the top or by immersing the entire pot, letting the excess water drain off. They can also be forced in hyacinth glasses.

Uses: Edging, cutting, bedding, forcing, companion plant.

Hyacinthus 'Anne Marie'

Hyacinthus 'City of Haarlem'

Indian shot; see **Canna**

Ipheion (i-FEE-on u–ni–FLOR–um) **spring starflower, H,** easy, SP. ○ ◑ 🐞 ❀
Height: 6 inches
Color: Bluish white
Zones: 6 to 10
Characteristics: This star-shaped flower is lovely lining a path where its stars will light the way at dusk. Over a period of several weeks, each bulb will send up many stems, each with a single, long-lasting flower. It has floppy, grassy leaves that appear in fall and stay all winter, disappearing only after the spring flowers have bloomed. The flowers are 1 inch across and have a minty fragrance while the foliage, if bruised, smells like peeled onions. Spring starflower is native to Peru and Argentina. *Ipheion uniflorum* 'Wisley Blue' stands 4 to 6 inches tall with lilac-blue flowers.
Cultural Information: Plant spring starflower bulbs 6 inches apart and 3 inches deep in well-drained soil. These bulbs multiply quickly, adapting to almost any condition, including clay soil. They prefer benign neglect, spurning fertilizer and adjusting to nature's rains whether plentiful or scarce.
Forcing Instructions: Spring starflower is a wonderful bulb for forcing indoors in winter. It blooms indoors with only four hours of direct sunlight when given night temperatures of 50° to 65°F and day temperatures of 68°F and above. Cover with 1 inch of soil and keep evenly moist until after the bloom ends and the foliage withers and dies. The pots can then be stored dry until it is time to repot and bring into bloom.
Uses: Potted plant, rock garden, naturalizing.

Iris; for information on *Iris*, see *Burpee American Gardening Series: Perennials*

Kafir lily; see **Clivia**

King's spear; see **Eremurus**

Lady's sorrel; see **Oxalis**

Lebanon squill; see **Puschkinia**

Leucojum (lew-KO-jum) **snowflake, H,** easy, SP. ○ ◑ 🌡 🐞 ❀
Height: 6 to 18 inches
Color: White
Zones: 3 to 8
Characteristics: The name *Leucojum* is from the Greek word for white violet and refers to the snowflake's sweet vanilla fragrance. The charming little bell-like flowers are pristine white with a green dot at the end of each petal and are borne on thin, graceful stems. It's very dainty, so plant it in groups of a dozen or more for an effective display. There is a spring snowflake (*L. vernum*) that blooms in early spring with the *Chionodoxa*, just after the snowdrop, and there is a summer snowflake (*L. aestivum*) that is the tallest variety and blooms in late spring with the tulip. The spring snowflake is only 6 to 9 inches high and a good companion for *Chionodoxa* species. The summer snowflake is 14 to 18 inches high with three to five bells nodding gracefully on its slender stems. It self-sows, so be careful to watch for the shining, narrow leaves of new seedlings.
Cultural Information: Snowflake, like most bulbs it seems, prefers well-drained, rich soil. Once

Below left: Ipheion *species blooming at the edge of pachysandra*

Below right: Leucojum aestivum

planted, it need not be disturbed for years. Set the bulbs 4 inches apart and cover them with 3 to 4 inches of soil. If they are planted late in fall, they may not bloom until their second year. Water them well after planting. Additional watering throughout their blooming season is seldom needed. It is a very undemanding bulb and long lived in the garden.

Uses: Cutting, background, companion plant, naturalizing.

Lilium (LIL-ee-um) lily, H, easy, SU. ○ ◑ ⬥ ✿

Zones: 4 to 8

Height: 2 to 7 feet

Colors: All except blue

Characteristics: The summer bulb of choice, lily ranks among the finest garden plants, providing exquisite form, glorious color and delightful fragrance. There are so many beautiful varieties of hardy garden lily that some of them should grace every garden. Lily is easy to grow and increases in beauty, size and the number of flowers from year to year. Lily makes splendid, often fragrant, flowers for arrangements. When cutting for this purpose, be sure not to remove more than one-third of the plant's foliage, lest the plant be weakened and its performance in future years be impaired. Lily is easy to grow in the garden for the first few years, but unless the soil conditions are to its liking it tends to die out.

Asiatic hybrids are named for their ancestors, and these elegant lilies are among the first to bloom in June and July and will take more shade than other lilies. They are easy to grow and increase quickly. They grow 2 to 5 feet tall with blooms 4 to 6 inches wide and are very hardy. 'Enchantment' is one of the most celebrated hybrid lilies, as popular today as it was in 1942 when it was introduced. It has upright clusters of vibrant orange flowers dusted with dark spots; each flower is 6 inches across. At 3 feet tall it doesn't need to be staked.

Commonly known as trumpet lilies, the regal Aurelians reign in stately elegance over the midsummer garden. These lilies are generally taller than the Asiatic hybrids, and they bloom later. Their height makes them especially useful at the back of a perennial border, where they add vertical interest and visual depth. Their perfume is always pleasant, never cloying. They make spectacular arrangements. They retain their color and vigor better if they receive just a half-day of sun, preferably in the morning. 'Black Dragon' is a magnificent lily, evolved from years of cross-breeding. The trumpets are immense, icy white inside with maroon exteriors, intensely fragrant and borne on towering 5- to 7-foot-tall stems. They are prolific bloomers, irresistible and unforgettable in the border.

Perhaps the most spectacular of all the lilies are the hybrids descended from species native to the Orient. They bloom later from August to September, when blooming flowers are at a premium. 'Stargazer' is an exceptionally free-blooming variety with crimson petals outlined with white. It is only 2 to 3 feet tall and rarely needs staking.

Tiger lilies, the easiest to grow, have large nodding blooms whose reflexed petals are splashed with the black dots that inspired their common name. In many areas of the country they have naturalized along roadsides and fields.

Not to be overlooked, species lilies are long-time favorites with old-fashioned charm and grace. It is known that they were first cultivated 3,500 years ago; representations appear on Cretan pottery dating from 1500

Lilium regale *(wonderfully fragrant in midsummer)*

Above: Lilium *'Black Dragon'*

Left: Lilium candidum

Above: Lilium *'Enchantment'*

B.C. The Madonna lily (*L. candidum*) is a classic June beauty with a sweet fragrance. Stately 3- to 4-foot stalks bear clusters of pure white blooms—a glorious sight with blue delphiniums.

The regal lily (*L. regale*) couldn't be more appropriately named. This classic lily is one of the parents of the Aurelian hybrids. Once established it will produce as many as 20 blooms on 4-foot stems in early summer. The trumpets are snowy white with yellow throats and lilac-pink exteriors. It suffuses the garden around it with delightful fragrance.

The meadow lily (*L. canadense*) is one of my favorites. It is tall with smaller, bell-shaped flowers that spread open and slightly turn up the tips of their petals. It comes in colors from yellow through orange to almost red and has purple freckles. I grow it in a moist, wooded area surrounded by the tall and delicate, tiny white flowers of *Thalictrum* (similar to baby's breath, on tall, 4-foot stems) where it blooms surrounded by a white mist.

The Turk's cap lilies are the robust sort and the American native *L. superbum* (I'd like to meet the horticulturist who named it) is no exception, with nodding flowers whose petals curve back so they are almost touching behind the flower's head.

Cultural Information: Unlike many other flower bulbs, the lily never becomes entirely dormant. It should be planted as soon as possible, while its roots are moist and pliable. Many varieties of lily do not die back enough to dig up until quite late in fall and therefore can't

be supplied until the middle of November or even early December. In areas where winter arrives early, prepare the soil in the proposed lily bed before the ground freezes and cover with a mulch of straw, salt hay, leaves or evergreen boughs. This will keep the ground from freezing so the bulbs can be planted upon arrival. Replace this covering after the ground has frozen hard.

The lily's first requirement is excellent drainage; heavy, waterlogged ground causes the bulbs to rot. It should never be planted in a location where water stands on the surface of the soil for long periods after a rain. Although the ideal situation for the lily is one where it will receive full sun on its head and shade on its ankles, the lily will succeed in either full sun or light, dappled shade. We recommend overplanting with a shallow-rooted groundcover, to keep the lily roots shaded and cool. Such conditions can be improved by working in generous amounts of compost, peat moss and well-rotted manure. The lily thrives in neutral or slightly acid soil. Space the bulbs 12 inches apart. The correct depth depends on bulb size and the type of soil. In light, sandy soil, the bulbs should be considerably deeper than in heavy clay soil. In general the top of the bulb should be 4 to 6 inches below the soil surface. It is better to plant a bulb too shallowly than too deeply; lily roots are contractile and can pull a bulb down to the ideal level, but can't push up a bulb too deeply set. The Madonna lily is an exception and should

be planted with the top of the bulb at the soil surface or, at most, an inch or two below; this is a dry-weather variety, native to the hot Mediterranean regions, and it needs sunlight and heat to do well in the garden. It is fairly dormant after flowering and must, therefore, be planted or moved in August or early September. This gives time for the bulbs to send up rosettes of leaves typical of this variety before the ground freezes. Other varieties are best planted in fall, although spring planting is acceptable and perhaps preferable in very cold areas where the ground freezes hard by November.

Bulbs planted in fall have more time in which to develop a good root system and, therefore, usually flower better than those set out in the spring. Most lily bulbs produce two sets of roots, one at the base of the bulb itself, and another at the top of the bulb where the new stem emerges. To accommodate both sets of roots, lilies are best planted more deeply than other bulbs. A good rule of thumb is to cover the bulb with soil to a depth of three times the length of the bulb. Dig a hole somewhat deeper and wider than necessary and partially refill the hole with loose, enriched soil. Set the bulb in gently with the roots spread as much as possible. Gradually fill in the hole with soil, firming it down as you go. After planting, water thoroughly and keep well watered for the first few weeks and during extended periods of drought thereafter. After flowering, remove the spent flowers so they do not set seed, which will weaken the plant and inhibit its future productivity. Allow the foliage to continue growing until it dies back naturally in the fall. Leave the lilies alone as long as they are doing well. After many years, if they become crowded, dig up and transplant them (Madonnas in August or early September and other varieties from mid-September to mid-October).

Forcing Instructions: If a heated greenhouse or southern sunny exposure is available, many lilies can be forced into flower during the winter or early spring. For this purpose, pot the bulbs as soon as they are available and grow them outdoors or indoors at a temperature of 60° to 70°F so that they will develop good root systems. Before frost, bring them into the greenhouse and keep them at 50°F, increasing the heat to 65°F when the buds show. This increase is not essential; a lower temperature merely slows the process and retards the flowering.

The new *L. × hollandicum* hybrids flower three weeks from the time the first bud is visible; others, in five to six weeks. Take care not to overwater the plants and to fertilize with a liquid fertilizer solution every other week until the buds are full-size. Once the flowers open, lower the temperature at night or remove the pots to a cooler room. At the lower temperature, most lilies will keep for several weeks.

Uses: Potted plants, middle to back of a border, naturalizing.

Lily; see *Lilium*

Lily of the field; see *Anemone*

Lily of the valley; see *Convallaria*

Lycoris (ly-KOR-is) **hardy amaryllis, magic lily, mystery lily, H,** easy, SU. ○ ◖

Zones: 5 to 10
Height: 1½ to 3 feet
Colors: Pink, lavender, red, white
Characteristics: Lycoris squamigera is sometimes called the magic, or mystery, lily because of its unique habit of growth. After a good soaking rain, the flowering stalks appear so quickly it is as if by magic. This delicately fragrant trumpet of a flower, 3 to 4 inches across that blooms in clusters of 8 to 12 flowers around the top of a tall leafless stem, and gives a soft, airy effect. The long, straplike, green leaves appear and disappear in June and/or July, a month or more before the flowers arrive in August and September. Care must be taken to mark the spot where the bulbs are located before the leaves are gone to prevent cultivating around the bulbs after the foliage dies down. It is easy to cut the flower stalk by mistake. Plantings of six or more bulbs are nice in drifts under groundcovers or between perennials where the bottom of their naked flower stem can be hidden. It also is terrific in the border when combined with *Anemone japonica* or another perennial that blooms at the same time and, if planted close by, can hide their bottom.

Cultural Information: Lycoris bulbs are available in fall and spring and can be planted at either time. Choose a place where the bulbs will not have

Lycoris squamigera

to be disturbed, because they make a permanent planting that blooms for many years. Planting in an open woodland among ferns makes a very attractive display, although it is equally attractive in beds and borders. Plant the bulbs as soon as you receive them, 5 inches deep and 6 inches apart, in humus-rich, well-drained soil. For fall planting in cold areas, give the bulbs a covering of strawy manure, leaves, salt hay or evergreen branches after the soil has frozen. For spring planting, if the bulbs arrive while the ground is still frozen, keep them in a cool, frost-free place, exposed to the air and without any covering. Plant as soon as the weather and soil conditions permit in well-drained, average soil. It needs normal moisture. Remove the faded flowers after they bloom. In cold areas use a straw mulch or evergreen branches for winter care. Sometimes it takes the bulbs more than a year to become well established and bloom, if the location is not exactly to their liking. Divide when overcrowded, right after the flower dies.

Uses: Cutting, bedding, potted plant, container plant.

Magic lily; see *Lycoris*

Mertensia (MER-ten-sia) **Virginia bluebells, H,** Native American, easy, SP. ○ ◑ ❗ ❀
Zones: 4 to 8
Height: 1 to ½ feet
Colors: Pink changing to blue
Characteristics: Virginia bluebell first opens with pink, nodding, bell-shaped flowers that, over its long bloom of a month or two, gradually change to blue. Often both pink and blue flowers are blooming together on the same stem, which is very attractive. It blooms with the late daffodils and continues on to welcome the tulips; it is a wonderful complement to both flowers and when planted between and around the different varieties, provides an easy transition from early to late spring bloom.

Virginia bluebell naturalizes and increases yearly in strength and in the number of flowers.

Muscari *species*

It will disappear almost as fast as it appears and there will be no trace of it in June. Its foliage disappears too quickly to be a noticeable eyesore.
Cultural Information: The roots of Virginia bluebell resemble thin brown twigs with small buds visible at various spots. It prefers to be planted in a moist, highly organic soil enriched with compost or peat moss. Plant the crowns 1 inch below the soil and 8 inches apart. Mulching with 2 to 3 inches of compost in fall will help to hold the moisture and provide all the nourishment the plant needs. Sometimes, the first year, it is dwarf with few blooms but as it becomes accustomed to its new home it will colonize and be beautiful indefinitely.
Uses: Naturalizing, woodland walk, borders.

Montbretia; see *Crocosmia*

Muscari (mus-KAR-ee) **grape hyacinth, H,** easy, SP. ○ ◑ ❀ ❀
Zones: 2 to 10
Height: 6 to 10 inches
Colors: White, shades of blue and purple
Characteristics: Grape hyacinth is an enchanting little flower that couldn't be more accommodating. Small and formal, it stands at attention in its peaked cap while sweetly scenting the air around it. You might think it was created just as a companion plant for daffodils and early tulips because the combinations are so delightful. On the other hand, it's spectacular when growing by itself in sweeping drifts. The flowers of the common grape hyacinth (*Muscari armeniacum*)

are 6-inch-tall spikes of bright, cobalt blue, tightly held bell-shaped flowers. 'Blue Spike' has fragrant, double, bright blue flowers 10 inches tall that are exceptionally long-lasting.

M. botryoides 'Album' is the white version with blossoms like tiny pearls—a charming companion for *Anemone blanda* or red species tulips. Not at all like the familiar grape hyacinth in appearance, the feather hyacinth (*M. comosum* 'Plumosum') is equally useful. The stalks are 8 to 10 inches tall with feathery blossoms of bright violet, a good combination with orange tulips. Any *Muscari* can be grown easily in less cultivated parts of the garden where it naturalizes with little care needed from the gardener. It doesn't need winter protection in even the coldest zones. When the flowers are gone, it can be rather untidy with its long leaves flopping over its neighbors. Unlike most bulbs, its foliage will stay all summer.
Cultural Information: Ordinary, well-drained soil is *Muscari*'s only requirement. Plant it 3 inches deep and 3 inches apart. It doesn't like fertilizers and expects normal water, rarely needing more than nature ordinarily provides but able to withstand considerably more. After the flowers die, let the foliage die back even though it takes some time; don't cut it. This plant is so undemanding, the clumps may be transplanted while in bloom. Left in the ground untended, it will rapidly increase to form a grasslike carpet. Sometimes it self-sows, producing seedlings that take three years to bloom.

Mertensia *species*

Forcing Instructions: Grape hyacinth blooms in winter, 12 weeks from planting. The plant emerges 2 to 3 weeks at 40° to 45°F. Use a 5- to 6-inch pot with good drainage material, broken crockery or pebbles, an inch deep in the bottom. Soil should be a mixture of one part planting formula or commercial soil to one part builders' sand or perlite and one part peat moss. Add ground limestone according to the package directions. No fertilizer is needed. Plant the bulbs 2 to 3 inches below the surface and 2 to 3 inches apart. Water the pots well before placing in cold storage to allow the roots to develop. Follow the directions for forcing on page 34.

Uses: Edging, cutting, naturalizing, rock garden, forcing, companion plant.

Mystery lily; see *Lycoris*

Naked lady; see *Amaryllis*

Narcissus (nar-SIS-sus) **daffodil, H,** easy, SP. ○ ◑ 🌡 ❀
Zones: 4 to 10
Height: 4 to 20 inches
Colors: Plain or bicolors of yellow, orange, pink, white
Characteristics: A gifted, large and varied family, among the most self-sufficient of bulbs; one could be quite content if this were the only spring bulb one grew. There is much confusion over the family's name. For all practical purposes, the names daffodil and *Narcissus* are interchangeable, daffodil being the English common name for the Latin classification of *Narcissus*.

We know of one grower with 4,000 different daffodils and

Narcissus *'Dutch Master' (giant trumpet daffodil)*

Narcissus triandrus *'Thalia'*

Narcissus poeticus *'Actaea'*

Narcissus *'Accent' (one of the loveliest pink daffodils)*

Narcissus *'Cheerfulness'* (double-flowered daffodil)

there are more than three times that number of registered varieties. If well planned, a naturalized daffodil planting, including early, mid- and late-season varieties, can last two to three months or longer. A turn-of-the-century garden writer said, "One could never have enough of such a rare gold."

The worldwide method of classifying daffodils as devised by the Royal Horticultural Society of England categorizes them by divisions numbered 1 to 11. These divisions define flower type, not quality. By understanding the different divisions you can begin to see the many possibilities of form and design for your garden.

Division 1: Giant trumpet daffodils have trumpets as long as, or longer than, the petals. They are the largest of all daffodils and among the first to bloom. 'King Alfred' is the best-known with its golden yellow, frilled trumpet and height of 18 inches. 'Spellbinder' is the reverse of the classic bicolor daffodil, with yellow petals and a trumpet that matures to white at the base.

Division 2: Large-cupped daffodils include some of the most striking and exquisite varieties. They usually bloom a little later than the giant trumpets. The cups are more than one-third as long as the perianth (outside) petal. The cups vary in size and shape, and in many varieties their colors contrast with the petals. 'Ice Follies' is a favorite with very large flowers that have fresh white petals and a shallow, fluted cup of primrose yellow that changes to ivory. 'Peaches and Cream' is an elegant pastel contrasted with a soft apricot-pink cup against silvery white petals.

Division 3: The small-cupped daffodils are distinguished by one flower to a stem, and the cup is not more than one-third the length of the perianth petals.

Division 4: Double daffodils have many central petals but don't form distinct cups or trumpets. The larger petals are, in some varieties, interspersed with shorter petals of a different color. 'Cheerfulness' is exactly that with its enchanting, creamy white rosettes in clusters of three or four blooms on a stem. It blooms late with a sweet fragrance.

Division 5: Triandrus comprise a charming group of daffodils and are noted for their airy grace. The petals are often curved back behind the cups like pretty wings. In most varieties the flowers are pendant, late flowering, and have a pleasing, fruity fragrance. All of the varieties are cluster flowered with two to six flowers on a stem. 'Thalia' is much loved for its graceful form and exquisite perfume. Its charming nodding flowers, the whitest of all daffodils, are 15 inches tall.

Division 6: The Cyclamineus hybrids are characterized by long trumpets and swept-back perianth petals that lend it a "cyclamen" look. 'Jenny', a dainty little daffodil 10 inches tall, flaunts her good looks by flipping her white petals back.

Division 7: Jonquilla hybrids, the most fragrant of all the daffodils, are hybrids of *N. Jonquilla*, and are typically bright yellow with several sweetly scented, short-cupped flowers on each stem. 'Pipit', 'Sugarbush' and 'Ziva Paperwhite' are excellent varieties.

Division 8: Tazetta hybrids, daffodils with cups distinctly shorter than the perianth, are very showy as they bloom in clusters of three to eight flowers on each stem. They have an alluring, musky fragrance. 'Geranium' is a superprolific and very fragrant daffodil with four to seven flowers on each stem. It has a white perianth centered with an orange cup.

Division 9: The Poeticus daffodils, the beloved pheasant's eye and poet's narcissus, are not unlike a dogwood blossom, with large white petals surrounding a small yellow cup rimmed with red. 'Actaea' is one of the best with blooms 3 inches across and blue-green foliage. It is delightfully fragrant and naturalizes very well. It is 17 inches tall and one of the last daffodils to bloom.

Division 10: The species and wild forms of daffodils are as nature made them, untouched by hybridizers. They are generally smaller and daintier than the hybrids and they are particularly at home in natural settings and in a rock garden. They include many unusual and appealing forms. My favorite is *N. Bulbocodium conspicuous* 'Yellow Hoop Petticoat', named for its wide, funnel-shaped cup and narrow petals. The flowers, blooming midseason, measure only an inch long and make a bright show when naturalized in fine grass. Their narrow, rushlike foliage appears in fall and is nearly evergreen, staying all winter. *N. asturiensis* is a tiny plant, only 4 inches tall, a perfect miniature of a yellow trumpet daffodil. It blooms in very early spring, often the last week of February in Zone 6.

Division 11: Split cup or "butterfly" daffodils are characterized by cups that are deeply split and gracefully spread against large perianth petals. For many gardeners they are among the most intriguing and beautiful of all daffodils. 'Palmares' is a favorite of mine for outstanding color and form. Its silky, white perianth petals set off a luxuriously ruffled collar of apricot-pink.

Cultural Information: Daffodils prefer light, well-drained soil, rich in humus. Work the soil a few inches deeper than is necessary to plant, in order to give the bulbs a prepared bed into which they'll send their delicate roots. The bulbs are planted 2 to 3 times as deep as their diameter. Normal moisture usually provided by spring and fall rains is all they require. Some tolerate wet soil conditions better than others. Divide the bulbs when the plants produce noth-

ing but foliage and replant in organically enhanced soil. Some varieties, 'February Gold', for example, increase more rapidly than others.

Forcing Instructions: With careful planning, daffodils can be forced to bloom indoors from December through April. They will emerge 8 to 12 weeks from the time they are planted. Plant several bulbs, spaced ½ inch apart, in a pot with good drainage. The taller varieties might need support. Add enough soil over the bulbs so just the tips are visible. The bulbs should be just below the rim of pot; do not press the bulbs into the soil. Water the pot thoroughly. See pages 34–36 for specific forcing instructions.

Uses: Edging, cutting, naturalizing, rock garden, bedding, forcing, potted plant, companion plant.

Ornithogalum (or-ni-THOG-a-lum) **star-of-bethlehem, H & T,** easy, SP. ○ ◑ ❚

Zones: 4 to 10 for *O. umbellatum*, 7 to 10 for *O. arabicum*
Height: 6 to 24 inches
Colors: White, yellowish white
Characteristics: The genus *Ornithogalum* consists of both hardy and tender bulbs and is a member of the lily family found in the wild around the Mediterranean. The flowers are grouped in umbels, or spreading clusters, on top of the stems. Each individual flower is star shaped with six petals. *O. umbellatum* is a short (6 to 8 inches tall), sleepy fellow, waking late on sunny days to open its flowers just before noon, and closing them early, well before dark. There is often a green stripe or

greenish coloration on the underside of the leaves that blends in with the slender leaves when the flowers are closed and makes them hard to find. Blooming a dozen or more on a stem, it is pretty when planted in a wooded or meadow area where it can spread and naturalize. In the fields of Israel *O. umbellatum* blooms profusely; perhaps that is why it was named the star-of-bethlehem. Its foliage appears in fall, stays all winter and disappears after the flowers bloom in the spring. In a small garden it multiplies so freely it can become a weed if not thinned regularly.

The nodding star-of-bethlehem, *O. nutans*, is 15 inches tall, with drooping spikes of green and white flowers attractive for arrangements. From a distance and in sunlight, a group of flowers appears to be silver-gray.

The star-of-bethlehem's taller cousin *O. arabicum* has fragrant flowers and is grown as a greenhouse plant. The 2-foot-high flowers are white with noticeable black pistils. All parts of the plant are poisonous.

Cultural Information: Ornithogalum is adaptable to almost any soil. Plant the bulbs 6 inches apart and 2 inches deep. If grown indoors the bulbs will bloom with a minimum of four hours of direct sunlight a day when given night temperatures of 50° to 60°F and day temperatures of 68° to 75°F. It must be potted up in fall and kept moist; fertilize regularly with a solution of liquid fertilizer throughout its growing cycle. Leaves appear soon after planting. The bulbs need a rest after their leaves die down in spring, when

Ornithogalum
thyrsoides

they should be allowed to dry out until it is time to replant in fall. The bulbs can be propagated in fall by removing the small bulbs that develop around the mother bulbs and growing them separately.

Uses: Naturalizing, woodland walk, potted plant.

Oxalis (ox-AL-is) **wood sorrel, lady's sorrel, H & T,** easy, SP. ○ ◑ ▮

Zones: 6 to 8
Height: 4 to 5 inches
Colors: Crimson, white, pink, yellow
Characteristics: Wood sorrel is a charming little plant ideal for growing indoors or outdoors, attractive even when not in bloom. The green leaves grow in neat mounds and are shaped like clover. Above the leaves the flat, open flowers are 1 inch across with five petals. The bulbs bloom in spring outdoors or fall indoors a few weeks after planting.

There are both winter blooming, tender varieties of *Oxalis* and summer blooming, hardy varieties. The winter varieties are planted in fall. In late spring they should begin their rest period. The summer-blooming varieties are planted in early spring and are used for potted plants or for bedding outdoors, then stored to rest over winter. Although virtually ever blooming, flower production is heaviest in the autumn and spring; in summer the plant tends to rest when temperatures exceed 85°F. Pink carpet (*O. adenophylla*) is a good outdoor variety with dainty, lilac-pink flowers blooming above neat mounts of silvery green foliage. It makes an attractive groundcover in a sunny, sheltered spot with good drainage. *O. Regnellii* makes a splendid indoor potted plant that couldn't be easier to grow. It obligingly produces a wide-spreading canopy of olive-green, shamrock-shaped leaves with purple undersides. A prolific bloomer, its clusters of dainty, starry, white flowers make for a pretty nosegay effect. It requires bright light (not direct sun) and plenty of moisture.

Cultural Information: Oxalis emerges one week after planting, if the temperatures are between 60° and 65°F. Plant 2 inches deep and 4 to 6 inches apart in well-drained, average soil. In fall after first frost, dig up the bulbs and bring them indoors. Spread them thinly in a dry place to cure, until they are dry and firm. They may be stored without any covering until planting time in spring; then, separate the bulb clusters to propagate new plants.

Forcing Instructions: For indoor pots, plant the bulbs not more than 1 inch deep in a fairly rich, porous soil mixture. Place three or four in a 4-inch pot, or six to eight in a 6-inch pot. Keep the soil evenly moist (not drenched) at all times. Grow in or near a window, in reasonably bright light but no direct sun. The temperature should be cool, between 55° to 65°F. Blooms will appear in a few weeks' time and should continue for several months. To have large flowers over a long growing period, apply a solution of liquid fertilizer about every other week throughout the growing season and remove any faded flowers. The bulbs require a rest period and should be allowed to dry off gradually after they have finished blooming. They can be left in the pots and stored in a cool, frost-free, dry spot. At the beginning of the next growing season, repot the new bulbs, which will have developed at the end of the long, stringlike roots.

Uses: Edging, rock garden, bedding, forcing, hanging basket.

Oxalis Regnellii

Pasque flower; see *Anemone*

Peacock orchid; see *Acidanthera*

Persian buttercup; see *Ranunculus*

Peruvian lily; see *Alstroemeria*

Peruvian scilla; see *Scilla*

Pineapple lily; see *Eucomis*

Poppy-flowered anemone; see *Anemone*

Puschkinia (push-KIN-ee-a) **blue puschkinia, striped** or **Lebanon squill, H,** easy, SP. ○ ◑ ✿

Height: 4 to 6 inches
Colors: Pale blue and white
Zones: 3 to 10
Characteristics: The little-known, blue puschkinia blooms with the early daffodils. Its delicate coloring is the faded blue and white of denim, with delicate stripes visible only when viewed up close. The fragrant, pale, 1-inch, nodding bells bloom above long, green, narrow leaves starting in March and staying through April; bloom lasts several weeks if the weather stays cool.

Puschkinia is a hardy soul, withstanding any weather but hail and high heat. It has a singular habit of blooming the moment the bud pushes through the ground. As the days progress the stem continues to grow up to its full height, blooming all the way. The foliage appears around the flowers and grows up with them. After the flowers fade, the foliage matures quickly, so this plant is good to naturalize in a lawn. I like to plant it above early daffodils so they bloom together, creating a sea of blue background for the daffodils' golden yellow trumpets.
Cultural Information: Any well-drained soil enriched with peat moss, leaf mold and ground lime is suitable for blue puschkinia. Plant them 2 to 3 inches apart and 2 to 3 inches deep. It has normal moisture requirements. There is no special care after the foliage fades and it can be left undisturbed for many years. Divide after the foliage withers and propagate from the small bulbs that develop around the larger ones. (The bulbs are so inexpensive most gardeners just buy additional bulbs.)
Forcing Instructions: Blue puschkinia will bloom indoors in early winter, 8 to 12 weeks after planting, at 35° to 45°F. Plant in a 6-inch-deep pot with good drainage. Fill the pot to 1½ inches below the rim with a rich planting formula. Set 6 to 12 bulbs in each pot spaced ½ inch apart. The bulbs' tops should be just below the rim of the pot. Cover the bulbs with ½ inch of soil and water well. Place the pot where the bulbs will receive indirect light.
Uses: Edging, cutting, naturalizing, rock garden, forcing, companion plant.

Quamash; see *Camassia*

Ranunculus (ra-NUN-kew-lus) **Persian buttercup, T,** difficult, SP. ○ ◑

Zones: 8 to 10
Height: 1 to 2 feet
Colors: Yellow, white, golden red, orange, pink, some ringed or tipped with deeper color
Characteristics: Ranunculus 'Tecolote Giants' has been described as delicate as tissue paper and as brilliant as a western sunset when the petals unfold in superb double and semidouble rosettes, 3 inches across. The aristocratic Tecolote strain, developed by California breeders, is more consistently double. It has more petals than others and is exceptionally vigorous, producing an abundance of bloom for many weeks with rosettes of green, finely divided foliage. It will bloom late winter or early spring if grown in a cool greenhouse or sun porch, three to four months after planting. Each plant will have several stems flowering at the same time and may produce as many as 75 flowers over 3 to 4 months of bloom.
Cultural Information: In the South, plant *Ranunculus* outside in fall for winter and spring bloom. North of Zone 8, start them indoors 4 to 5 weeks before the last spring frost and transfer them to the garden for spring and early summer bloom. Anyone who wishes to grow fine specimens of *Ranunculus* should remember a few essentials of its culture: heavy feeding, constant moisture, good drainage and cool temperatures. It likes the soil around its stems dry, the soil around its roots moist—a tricky combination, but if the soil is mounded an inch over the bulbs, that inch of soil will dry out quickly yet help to hold the moisture around the bulbs' roots.

Ranunculus "bulbs" are among the strangest looking of all, resembling a tiny bunch of petrified bananas. Soak them overnight or for a few hours in water at room temperature, then plant. The tubers are really clumps of

Puschkinia *species*

Ranunculus *species*

enlarged roots, and should be planted with the points down so that the top is approximately 2 inches below the surface. They should be spaced about 6 inches apart.

The ideal soil for *Ranunculus* is very similar to that for *Anemone:* sandy loam heavily enriched with any kind of well-rotted manure and ground lime. However, it will grow well in practically any kind of soil provided it gets a good supply of water, good drainage, and some additional feeding. When the growth reaches approximately 2 or 3 inches, make small trenches between the plants and sprinkle in a teaspoonful of either cottonseed meal or fish meal (both are natural fertilizers available from nurseries or mail-order catalogs) per plant. This dose can be repeated six to eight weeks later, when the buds are beginning to appear; after this no additional feeding is necessary. If more practical, a complete, slow-release fertilizer may be applied, according to manufacturer's directions, when the roots are planted and again each fall.

Where mild winters prevail, the planting time extends from September to December. The earlier it is planted, the larger the specimens will develop. Later plantings are usually forced by spring warmth into quick growth and bloom without being able to form large plants. Farther north, where it is still hardy, planting should be delayed to October or early November to prevent early top growth, which would be killed during the winter. Only a light mulch should be used, as a heavy one would smother it.

In regions of severe winters, the tubers are planted in spring as soon as the ground becomes sufficiently warm and frost-free, or it may be started in a cold frame in February. Blooming during the summer, as it does by these methods, it must be given some protection from the hot sun. Divide the tubers in spring after the bloom has stopped and the foliage has withered.

Forcing Instructions: In the North, *Ranunculus* is most useful as a greenhouse or sunroom plant where it thrives with good drainage and a night temperature of 40° to 50°F. The plant emerges a few weeks after planting. Planted in late October, it will bloom in February and March. Use a 6-inch pot with a rich potting soil, with peat moss added to ensure the soil will stay moist without being soggy. Good drainage is very important because crowns must be kept dry and roots moist. Bottom-water the plant by placing the pot in a pan with several inches of water and letting it sit until the plant has taken up enough water to be moist all the way up to an inch below its surface. Plant 6 to 8 bulbs in each pot, 2 inches deep, and space 1½ inches between the bulbs and the edge of the pot. Remove any faded flowers to encourage further flowering. The flowers may need support. The foliage should be allowed to ripen after blooming; then, the tubers should be lifted and stored in a cool, dry place (50° to 55°F) until the next planting season.

Uses: Cutting, rock garden, bedding, forcing, potted plant, greenhouse.

Scilla (SIL-a) **squill, spring beauty, Peruvian scilla, H, easy, SP.** ○ ◑ ✿

Height: 4 to 6 inches
Colors: Blue, white
Zones: 1 to 8
Characteristics: One of the earliest *Scilla* to bloom is Siberian squill (*S. siberica*). 'Spring Beauty' is an improved, slightly larger variety than the common species with intense blue, nodding, star-shaped flowers

Scilla siberica *'Spring Beauty'*

on stems 4 to 6 inches high. It is one of the few bulbs that thrives in the low light under evergreen shrubs. It blooms in April and lasts three weeks or more. The ribbonlike foliage matures quickly, making this a good plant for the front of the border or planting in a lawn. *S. Tubergeniana* is white with blue pinstripes down the center of each petal. *S. peruviana*, Peruvian scilla, is a tender species recommended for forcing. *S. amethystina*, 8 to 10 inches high, blooms in May with a lovely amethyst color.

Cultural Information: All *Scilla* love a shady place, blooming happily even under a pine or other evergreen trees and shrubs. It is undemanding and lasts for years, increasing rapidly. It prefers the rich, well-drained soils of woodlands and dislikes fertilizer. Plant the bulbs 2 to 3 inches deep and 3 to 6 inches apart. It has average moisture requirements and can be divided in summer or fall. Because it is inexpensive, most people buy fresh bulbs to use in new settings.

Forcing Instructions: For indoor culture use a good planting formula. No fertilizer should be added. Keep the soil moist during the plant's active growth. Follow the instructions for forcing on page 34. The bulbs need a cool, dark place to develop their roots for 8 to 10 weeks before moving into indirect light. After flowering, gradually withhold water to dry off the bulbs, and store for the summer or plant out into the garden. Pots can be put on their sides for a 2-month dormant period and then started up again in the fall, when they should be watered well and gradually returned to a sunny window with indirect light. Divide the bulbs when repotting.

Uses: Cutting, naturalizing, rock garden, bedding, companion plant.

Scilla campanulata; see *Endymion*

Scilla hispanica; see *Endymion*

Shooting star; see *Dodecatheon*

Snow crocus; see *Crocus*

Snowdrop; see *Galanthus*

Snowflake; see *Leucojum*

Sorrel, lady's; see *Oxalis*

Sorrel, wood; see *Oxalis*

Spanish squill; see *Endymion*

Spring beauty; see *Scilla*

Spring crocus; see *Crocus*

Spring starflower; see *Ipheion*

Squill; see *Scilla*

Squill, Lebanon; see *Puschkinia*

Squill, Spanish; see *Endymion*

Squill, striped; see *Puschkinia*

Star lily; see *Erythronium*

Star-of-bethlehem; see *Ornithogalum*

Striped squill; see *Puschkinia*

Summer hyacinth; see *Galtonia*

Sword lily; see *Gladiolus*

Trout lily; see *Erythronium*

Tulip; see *Tulipa*

Top: Tulipa *'Burpee's Masterpiece Mixture' (Rembrandt)*

Above: Tulipa *'Angelique' (Double late)*

Tulipa tarda *(species)*

Tulipa *'Greenland'*
(Viridiflora)

Tulipa *'Queen of
Sheba' (lily-flowered)*

Tulipa (TOO-lip-a) **tulip, H,** easy, SP. ○

Zones: 3 to 7

Height: 3 to 30 inches

Colors: Bicolors and plain in all shades of white, pink, red, orange, purple, yellow

Characteristics: Everyone knows the tulip family for its gorgeous garden stars, the hybrids blooming in late spring. But its lesser-known ancestors, the species tulips, quietly blooming much earlier, are not well known. They are never as ostentatious as their city cousins but they share their quiet beauty at a time when the garden is bare. The species tulips, the country cousins, are woodland dwellers, growing in the sun under trees and disappearing before the trees leaf-out and shade them. The trees protect them from the sun in summer, keeping them dry and cool. They are delicate bulbs that can't be planted in perennial gardens where aggressive plants will spread and overrun them. If happy, they increase rapidly and flower generously.

Garden size and scale are important with wild tulips. Place them where they won't be dwarfed in a rock garden, lining a path, or massed in large number under trees.

If tulips from each of the different classifications described below are grown, you can have tulips blooming for approximately two months. The classifications are listed according to the order in which they come into bloom. Although they start at different times, many varieties will overlap and bloom at the same time.

Waterlily tulips (*T. Kaufmanniana*) are the earliest blooming of all tulip hybrids, often beginning in late March or early April, and they generally range from 6 to 8 inches tall. The flowers open wide, like waterlilies, and close each evening, often continuing their display for more than two weeks. Their leaves may be streaked or mottled with maroon. They provide a brilliant show in a border, a woodland or a rock garden.

Along with species tulips, the "single early" tulips are early to bloom. Of medium height, they are especially graceful and many are pleasantly fragrant. 'Princess Irene' is an unusually colored single early tulip. Its petals are soft shades of salmon and orange, with graceful flames of muted vermilion along the midribs. This is one of the most dependable tulips for forcing.

The "double early" tulips bloom at the same time as the single earlies but are showier with their layers of petals. 'Fringed Beauty' is a good variety.

The species tulips are the "original" tulips, tulips as they occurred naturally. They're star performers in the garden. Although small, 3 to 8 inches high, they will delight you with their bright colors, contrasting centers and graceful shapes. Often they are longer lived than other tulips; given full sun and a very well drained location, they'll bloom beautifully for years. Proof that size isn't everything! One of the most popular is known as *T. tarda*, technically renamed *T. dasystemon*. Just 3 inches tall, it produces clusters of three to six lovely, bright yellow and white, star-shaped flowers that open almost flat—perhaps the easiest to grow and the longest lived of all tulip species, even reseeding in some gardens.

T. Clusiana, another species tulip sometimes called the "peppermint-stick tulip," is one of the oldest in cultivation, dating to 1606 or earlier. Named for the botanist Clusius, who did much to popularize tulips in Europe, it has long, narrow flowers with white petals, striped with cheery red lines, on 14-inch stems.

The Fosterana tulips are the earliest-blooming class of tulips. Their spectacularly large, satiny blooms are borne on strong stems. They tend to be longer-lived than most, especially when planted deeply, and are perfect grouped as accents in the April garden or interplanted with such groundcovers as *Vinca minor*. 'Red Emperor' is one of the most famous *T. Fosterana*, with long, gleaming, scarlet petals with black bases, edged with yellow. These huge flowers are dramatic whether open on a sunny day or closed.

The Greigii tulips are the later-blooming versions of the waterlily tulip (*T. Kaufmanniana*), from which they have been hybridized. The flower colors are brightly orchestrated and their attractive foliage is mottled and splashed with bronze and maroon.

The triumph tulips bloom in mid-tulip season and bridge the gap between the early kinds and the last great burst of tulip bloom. 'Garden Party' with its white petals and dramatic, deep border of vivid rose along the edges is a striking and unusual bicolor.

The Darwin hybrids are among

the largest and the most spectacular of all the tulips, the product of a cross between 'Red Emperor' (*T. Fosterana*) and a number of single late tulips. They bloom in late midseason, with extralarge, long-lasting flowers on sturdy stems.

The "single late" group includes those that used to be called "Darwin," "Cottage" and "Breeder" tulips. The flowers are large, but slightly smaller that the Darwin hybrids, standing up better in bad weather. 'Queen of the Night' is unusual for its dark color, the breeders' attempt to achieve a black flower. It is a rich, deep purple-black suffused with steel blue and is a great complement to pink tulips.

Sometimes called "peony-flowered" tulips, the "double late" tulips provide a particularly full look when massed in the garden. They are wonderful for arrangements and are especially long lasting.

With their urn-shaped blooms and gracefully reflexing petals, the lily-flowered tulips are among the most refined and graceful. They bloom in early to mid-May in Zone 6, the blossoms opening in a star shape to fill a garden with elegant color. Lily-flowered tulips have been considered the epitome of tulip beauty for centuries. 'Marilyn' is an excellent choice.

The fringed tulips are distinguished by beautiful form, with finely laciniated (fringed) petals, as if each were edged with delicate fringe. On sunny days, the fringe catches and plays with the light. 'Aleppo' is red outside, golden apricot with fuchsia-purple inside.

The "bouquet" tulips have from three to five blooms on a stem in shades of red, yellow and pink. 'Happy Family' is a good variety.

The "parrot" tulips are exotic beauties, almost like orchids, with jagged petal edges and fascinating shapes, and are often tinted with green on the undersides. They are especially effective in arrangements. 'Flaming Parrot' is bold and exotic with its broad, gracefully twisted petals of brilliant yellow with crimson flames above a golden base, all accented by blackish purple anthers. When a virus is deliberately induced to infect Darwin tulips, they "break" into colorful variations called "Rembrandt" tulips. (When color is split into stripes or blotches, the flower is called "broken," or rectified.) These tulips were once the delight of 17th-century European tulip fanciers and the much-loved subjects of early Dutch painters. Each tulip is flamed with combinations of scarlet, plum, white, bronzy yellow and cream on approximately 20-inch stems.

The Viridiflora group of tulips has some of the loveliest and most unusual color combinations in the tulip world. The flowers are streaked with green, and the petals are often attractively fluted or serrated. They vary somewhat in height (15 to 24 inches) and length of bloom period, and each is uniquely beautiful. 'Greenland' has large, wavy petals of intense pink, striped with bright green and edged with gold.

Cultural Information: Well-drained, light, rich humus is the best soil for tulips. They

are also fond of lime. Holland Bulb Booster scattered on top of soil at the rate recommended by the manufacturer, watered in at planting time and every fall thereafter, is helpful. Water very well to start their roots growing in fall, after which they have normal water requirements. However, they are best replaced every year if the same number of bulbs is wanted, as for a formal planting—except species types or the Darwin hybrids if deeply planted (see page 74)—and if you want to be sure of the bloom returning in full splendor. Divide only when leaves are produced. After foliage dies down, dig up the bulbs, clean them up and replant them in fall, preferably in an area where tulips have not grown for three years. Unlike other bulbs, which increase by producing offsets annually, tulip bulbs split into smaller bulbs at maturity. These "half-bulbs" must then be grown for two to three years until they reach flowering size. Tulip bulbs mature and split more slowly when they are planted more deeply than is normally recommended. If you cover the Darwin hybrids, for example, with at least 8 inches of soil, you can expect flowers for as many as six or eight years. Leave them in place as long as they continue to bloom. When the bulbs send up leaves and no flowers, they need to be lifted, divided and preferably reset in a part of the garden where tulips have not grown for at least three years.

Wild tulips—species varieties —need dry summers. They can't be planted beside garden thugs, the aggressive plants that spread and choke out the more delicate flowers. If they are happy they will increase rapidly and flower generously. Plant them 3 to 6 inches deep and 3 to 6 inches apart.

Forcing Instructions: Tulips bloom in winter or early spring, about 16 weeks after planting. The plants emerge eight weeks after planting at 35° to 45°F. Use a 4- to 5-inch pot with good drainage. Tulips like well-drained, light, rich potting soil with peat moss mixed in. Plant them at a depth of 2 to 3 inches so their tops are just below the soil line, and space them ½ inch apart. Plant six bulbs to a pot for a full look. Water them thoroughly either from the top or by immersing the entire pot in a tub of water and letting the excess drain out the bottom. Single earlies and species types work best.

Uses: Edging, cutting, naturalizing, rock garden, bedding, forcing, potted plant, companion plant.

Turk's cap lily; see *Lilium*

Virginia bluebells; see *Mertensia*

Wild hyacinth; see *Camassia*

Windflower; see *Anemone*

Winter aconite; see *Eranthis*

Wonder flower; see *Ornithogalum*

Wood hyacinth; see *Endymion*

Zantedeschia *species*

Wood sorrel; see *Oxalis*

Yellow allium; see *Allium*

Zantedeschia (zan-te-DES-kee-a) **calla lily, T,** easy. ○ ◑ ▮ ✿.
Height: 18 inches
Colors: White, pink, yellow
Zones: 8 to 10
Characteristics: Large, elegant, and trumpet-shaped, calla lily flowers are gorgeous as cut flowers in arrangements and wedding bouquets, beautiful planted in a shady garden or grown in containers. In frost-free areas, calla lilies thrive in the garden in a moist, semi-shady place, and can be left in the ground year 'round. In other areas callas are grown indoors during the winter in a greenhouse or sunny window. They are suitable for a semi-shady spot in the yard during the summer, and thrive in a moist, yet well-drained place. They give off a slight, pleasant fragrance from the large flowers, 6 to 8 inches across. The arrow-shaped foliage is plain green or green spotted with white.

Cultural Information: For winter bloom indoors the tubers are planted in the fall. It takes 4 to 5 months for callas to bloom. They require rich, well-drained soil; one part loam, one part sand and one part compost, well rotted manure or peat moss is a good combination. One teaspoonful bonemeal per 6-inch pot of soil is also beneficial. Put a layer of pebbles or other drainage material in the bottom of pots and plant tubers in the potting mixture so that they are just below the surface. Plant the rhizomes individually in 6-inch pots, or several in a larger pot, to start their growth. Water well and keep in a cool place until roots have formed. When roots develop, move to a sunny, cool place. Callas grow best at night temperatures of 50° to 60°F and daytime temperatures at 68°F or warmer. Water daily and apply liquid fertilizer every week as soon as the buds are visible. After considerable growth has occurred it may be necessary to shift the plants to larger pots. If given proper growing conditions, each tuber should produce several flowers. Plants may not bloom if grown with poor indoor light, if the soil is not rich or moist enough, and if the tubers have not had a dormant period.

For summer bloom outdoors, callas are started inside in January or later and grown under cool conditions until outdoor planting time. After the last frost, transfer to rich, moist but well-drained soil in a semi-shady spot in the garden. For good results water thoroughly during dry weather and feed with a slow-release fertilizer.

Callas require a six- to eight-week, dry dormant period after flowering. Plants started in fall should have water gradually withheld beginning in May or June, and should be completely dry in several weeks. Leave bulbs in pots and store them on their sides in a cellar or other cool, dark place for dormancy, after which the tubers can be replanted in fresh soil and started into growth again. Callas grown in the garden must be lifted before frost and rested during the winter, as outlined above. Divide rhizomes in late summer or fall.

Uses: Cutting, bedding, forcing, pot plant, greenhouse

PESTS AND DISEASES

The most important step in dealing with pests and diseases is prevention. Grow healthy bulbs by taking the time to prepare the soil properly. The old saying, "Put a dollar plant in a five-dollar hole" is the key to a healthy, long-lived bulb. Healthy bulbs, like healthy people, are less susceptible.

Here are six basic steps to a healthier garden:

1. Properly prepare your garden the first year and replenish it yearly with compost, adding an inch or two on top of the soil.
2. Choose the right bulb for the right place. Don't force a bulb meant for a sunny location into a shady corner. If planted in the wrong place, a bulb becomes stressed and easily succumbs to disease.
3. Use a soaker hose or drip irrigation for watering. Overhead watering encourages fungus diseases.
4. Learn which insects are beneficial. Invite them to stay in your garden by providing them with conditions they like.
5. Check your plants regularly, especially the undersides of leaves, for any sign of pests. If you notice a problem, act quickly to discover the cause and prevent further damage.
6. Keep the garden clean. Never let debris spend the week, or even the night, if you can help it. It is an open invitation to insects, slugs and mice. Don't give them a home.

REASONS BULBS CEASE FLOWERING

◆ Bulbs did not receive enough water in fall while forming their roots.
◆ The foliage has been cut off before it ripened to provide the bulb with stored food.
◆ Lack of nutrients in the soil deprived the bulb. Add a topdressing of compost in fall and a slow-release fertilizer. Both, when watered well into the soil, will work their way down to the bulb's roots by spring when the bulb needs to replenish its food for the following year.
◆ Insufficient light on the ripening foliage will prevent photosynthesis, basic to plant life. Photosynthesis is the formation of complex food, fats and proteins, by action of light on chlorophyll, and it is critical for next year's bloom. Check to see if the trees or shrubs prevent sunlight from reaching the bulbs; perhaps a little pruning will correct the problem.
◆ Bulbs purchased from a garden center or farm stand where they have been exposed to temperatures of 70°F or higher will have diminished or no bloom. Buy your bulbs early. If you order from a mail-order catalog like Burpee, the bulbs come to you directly from cold storage.
◆ Poor drainage is one of the most common causes of lack of bloom. Bulbs rot in wet soil over winter.
◆ Bulbs may be eaten by mice or other animals (see page 81).

GET ACQUAINTED WITH YOUR GARDEN'S FRIENDS

Green lacewing

Ladybug

Praying mantis

Earthworms, bees, toads, green lacewings, ladybugs, praying mantises and trichogramma wasps are all garden friends. The earthworm tills and improves the soil while bees pollinate our bulbs, helping them increase in number. The ladybugs, green lacewings, trichogramma wasps, toads and praying mantises eat enemy insects. Helpful insects are available from your Burpee catalog.

Pest and Disease Controls

When pests or disease appear, we at Burpee recommend using safe, biodegradable, organic cures—not chemicals. Chemicals can linger in the soil, causing long-term damage by indiscriminately killing beneficial and harmful bacteria and insects alike. Always use safe garden controls first. Try the Ringer and Safer products available at your local garden center or through the Burpee catalog. It is unlikely that you will be bothered by many pests if you follow the steps for prevention carefully. Here are the most common pests and diseases:

APHIDS: These small, pear-shaped, sucking insects, often greenish white, red or black (but sometimes taking on the color of the plant), gather on the most tender plant parts—usually new growth and the underside of leaves. They suck plant sap, causing foliage to wither, resulting in a general loss of vigor.

They range from barely visible to 1/6 inch long. You will not have trouble seeing them, though, because they enjoy family picnics, attaching to a plant in groups.

Aphids can carry disease. Worse, they secrete a sweet, sticky substance called "honey dew," which attracts ants and promotes the growth of a fungus known as "Black Sooty Mold." The mold interferes with leaf function, slows photosynthesis and reduces the plant's vigor.

Prevention: Aphids are such a common pest they are almost a given. A large ladybug population will help keep them at bay.

Solutions: Sometimes a fairly strong spray from a hose on the underside of leaves will eliminate these pests. Control with Safer's Insecticidal Soap with a natural- and biodegradable-insecticide formula. Call in aphids' natural enemies: ladybugs, green lacewings and trichogramma wasps.

Aphids

Japanese beetle

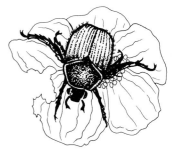

Beetle

JAPANESE BEETLES AND OTHERS: Today, Japanese beetles are the bane of gardeners east of the Mississippi, and they are spreading West. They'll eat almost anything: leaves, flowers, grass and fruit. No part of the plant is safe from beetles. They chew the stems, leaves and flowers, leaving good-size holes in the leaves. After 30 to 40 days of life as adult beetles, they lay their eggs in the soil. There the larvae hatch and eat the roots of plants and grass for approximately four months before hibernating for the winter. The next summer they emerge as beetles to continue the attack on the plant kingdom.

Prevention: Eliminate these destructive pests while they are living in the lawn or garden by using Safer Grub Killer. This powder contains spores of bacteria (*Bacillus popillae*, milky spore disease) toxic only to Japanese beetles and other grubs. It will not harm beneficial insects or pets, and is absolutely safe to handle and easy to use. Best of all, it is a long-lasting measure; the spores remain active in the soil for 10 years.

Solutions: You can buy beetle traps at garden supply stores. They lure beetles with a natural sex attractant plus a floral scent. The beetles fly into the trap and can't get out. Another good, homemade trap is a jar of water covered by a thin film of oil or soap suds. You can flick the slow-moving beetles off plants into the jar, and they won't be able to fly out.

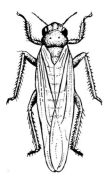

Leafhopper

LEAFHOPPERS: Wedge-shaped, small, and green, gray or yellow in color, leafhoppers suck juices from the plant and leave it with discolored, yellow leaves, stunted growth and buds that don't blossom. They are also carriers of plant diseases.

Prevention: Ladybugs, green lacewings and praying mantises love leafhoppers for dinner.

Solutions: Use an insecticidal soap, early in the day when the insects are less active.

Mite

Red spider mite

MITES: Eight-legged and borderline microscopic, mites are easily located by their webs on the undersides of leaves. Mites suck moisture and chlorophyll from the leaves, leaving them yellow and wrinkled.

Prevention: A forceful spray of water directed at the underside of leaves (done weekly), will control the mites.

Solutions: Spray or rub with a soapy solution. Safer's Insecticidal Soap is best, but 2 tablespoons of dishwashing soap can be mixed with 1 gallon of water and used carefully, if washed away completely after treatment to avoid damaging the leaves. Repeat every few days until mites are gone.

WHITEFLY: Whiteflies grow to 1/16 inch and have white wings large for their size. They suck the plant leaves, which turn yellow and eventually fall off. They are more a problem with indoor forced bulbs than in the garden where a good breeze will blow these pests away.

Prevention: Good spacing as specified for the plant variety should be provided when planting, so that air can circulate.

Solutions: Yellow pest strips coated with oil are available that attract whitefly; they stick to them and can't move. This is a fairly effective and pleasant way to control numbers of whiteflies if you can manage to hang the strips discreetly out of sight.

Whiteflies

Leaves damaged by the following pests, from left: beetles, flea beetles, caterpillars, aphids, and leafhoppers.

Slug

Snail

SLUGS AND SNAILS: Easy to spot, snails grow to 1½ inches and slugs to 5 inches long. The difference is that snails are clothed with a shell and slugs are naked. They sport the same colors: black, brown, gray or yellow. Both attack the foliage of plants and chew holes in the leaves. They also leave a tell-tale trail of silvery slime as they move.

Prevention: A ring of wood ashes, coarse sand, diatomaceous earth (coarse material made from silica-rich diatom shells) or limestone around the plants will keep both snails and slugs away because they don't like crawling over scratchy surfaces. Diatomaceous earth is used in swimming pool filters and is readily available at swimming pool supply stores.

Solution: A bowl of beer, even stale beer, set in the ground with the rim at or slightly below soil level will entice and drown them.

POWDERY MILDEW: This is a fungus disease, marked by the appearance of white, powdery areas on leaves. The oldest leaves are usually affected first and may wither and die. Powdery mildew winters-over in the South and is spread northward by winds. It flourishes in high temperatures.

Prevention: Avoid overhead watering, especially in late afternoon, unless absolutely needed.

Solutions: Control with sulfur dust and lime sulfur sprays.

BOTRYTIS BLIGHT: Another name for botrytis blight is gray mold blight, which gives a pretty good description of what to look for.

Prevention: Caused by humid conditions, it can be controlled by good air circulation, good sanitation and prompt removal of any diseased part to avoid spreading.

Solution: Safer's garden fungicide can be used as a treatment.

THRIPS: Thrips are tiny insects, ⅒ to ⅟₂₅ inch long, and they vary in color from yellow through brown to black. Despite their small size they can do a lot of damage. Their mouths are designed for piercing, and they damage plants by sucking their juices, leaving scarred leaves. As if this were not enough they also spread disease from one plant to another.

Solutions: Control by dusting the plant with tobacco dust or 1% Rotenone dust. Both are made from natural substances.

It is not always easy to identify the culprit of your garden's problems. If you are having trouble, mail or take a sample to your local nursery or county's Cooperative Extension Service agent of the USDA.

Animals in the Garden

Bulbs are a tasty treat to many animals during the dark days of winter when food is scarce. Mice, rabbits, squirrels and deer are the most common villains. Here is a list of ways to deal with the problem:

- Plant only poisonous bulbs that animals instinctively will not eat. Daffodils have the largest variety of sizes and shapes. With careful planning and planting of early-, mid- and late-season varieties it is possible to have 2 to 2½ months of bloom. In addition, *Colchicum, Caladium, Fritillaria,* calla lilies, snowdrops, belladonna lilies and *Allium* are all safe from animals.

- Deeper planting of bulbs can discourage mice from digging, but make sure you have good drainage.

- Edible bulbs can be planted in a cage of ½-inch wire mesh. Fold the mesh around a group of bulbs with plenty of soil and wire it closed to keep the animals from touching the bulbs.

Natural Solutions for Fighting Pests and Diseases

Mother Nature, in her system of checks and balances, has provided us with many plants that can be used as sources of insecticides and bacterial agents for fighting harmful insects. Bacillus thuringiensis (Bt): It is sold under the trade names of Ringer Attack and Thuricide. When eaten by caterpillars, it paralyzes their digestive system; it doesn't harm birds, bees, pets or humans.

Bacillus popillae or milky spore: This is found in Ringer Grub Attack. It kills by infecting grubs with milky spore disease, caused by Bacillus popillae. Infected grubs stop feeding and die, releasing billions of new spores to kill other grubs. A single application provides 10 or more years of control.

Insecticidal soaps: Biodegradable insecticides in liquid soap concentrate are safe and effective. Safer's has a line of soaps for different purposes.

The ladies in Burpee's customer service department answering mail at the turn of the century.

GARDENERS' MOST-ASKED QUESTIONS

The first Burpee catalog was mailed in 1876, and the catalogs have been coming ever since, offering gardeners a wealth of seeds, flowering plants, fruits, shrubs and trees as well as advice for better gardening. From the earliest years, Burpee has received letters from customers describing their gardens and asking for help with the problems they encounter. Here are the most frequently asked questions concerning bulbs.

DESIGN AND PLANNING

Q: Which bulbs grow in shade?
A: Many early-flowering bulbs grow well in partial shade if planted under deciduous trees. They will be in full sun during much of their growth period because the tree will not have leafed-out yet. Try *Chionodoxa*, crocus, *Eranthis*, *Erythronium*, *Fritillaria*, *Galanthus*, *Iris reticulata*, *Leucojum vernum*, lily of the valley, *Muscari*, tulips, daffodils, *Scilla siberica* and wood hyacinth. Summer-blooming bulbs or foliage bulbs that can tolerate shade include tuberous begonia, *Caladium* and lily. *Colchicum* and *Lycoris* are fall-blooming bulbs that can grow in partial shade.

Q: Which bulbs last longest in the garden without having to be dug up every year?
A: Daffodils last a long time. Tulips deteriorate fairly quickly, with some exceptions. Species tulips last, and some "perennial" tulips have been selected among Darwin types for their longevity. Refer to the list of bulbs for naturalizing, page 18.

Q: Which bulbs are considered deer-proof?
A: All the bulbs that are poisonous. These include daffodil, snowflake, iris, *Scilla siberica* and *Fritillaria*.

Q: How can bulbs be combined with perennials?
A: Choose the bulbs and perennials with care. Plant the bulbs in front of, around or behind the perennials, rather than directly on top of them. Make sure the perennials do not shade the bulb foliage, which must die back naturally, but design your beds in such a way that the perennials hide the dying bulb foliage from view. See also page 18.

GROWING

Q: *When can I cut back the foliage on my bulbs?*
A: The foliage of spring-blooming bulbs can take several weeks longer to die back than the flowers. Be patient! As long as the foliage is green, it is using sunlight to make food to store in the bulb. Landscape around the dying foliage with taller perennials or annuals. Do not tie up the leaves of the bulbs, but allow the maximum leaf surface to be available to the sun's rays.

Q: *I have to move my spring-blooming bulbs. When is a good time to do this?*
A: Any time in spring is good if you are careful to dig a large enough root ball so as not to disturb the threadlike roots. It is best, though, to wait until the foliage dies back naturally. Their dormancy period is during the summer, not the winter. If you cannot plant right away, hold the bulbs cool and dry until fall, then plant in the desired location.

Q: *I want to store my bulbs over the summer because we are moving. How shall I do this?*
A: Dig up the bulbs and allow them to dry in a cool, shaded location, such as a back porch. Remove any soil. Store them in nylon stockings, or spread them in dry peat moss or vermiculite in a box with vented sides. Try to avoid the bulbs touching each other. Store them, if possible, at about 50°F.

Q: *Do bulbs have to be divided?*
A: Over time, such bulbs as daffodils, lilies and *Colchicum* can become crowded and stop blooming. They should be divided after the foliage dies back; dig them up then, and gently break them apart. It is best to replant immediately. The smaller bulbs may take one or two years to bloom. Hybrid tulips call for division almost every year as they will stop blooming or produce poorer quality blooms if left alone. Planting them more deeply will also help improve their longevity; see page 75.

Q: *How late can I plant spring bulbs?*
A: Spring-blooming bulbs begin growing roots in fall. Try to plant all bulbs except tulips as soon as possible after you receive them to allow for maximum root growth. Tulips are best planted after October 15; see pages 74–76. You can plant until the ground freezes, as long as you can work the soil. The bulbs will not perform as well the first year if they are planted very late; try to plant at least a few weeks before frost.

Q: *How can I store my dahlia tubers over the winter? My begonias, cannas, gladiolas?*
A: For dahlias, gladiolas and cannas, allow the foliage to be blackened by the first killing frost. Begonias should be dug up right before the first frost. Allow the bulbs to dry away from direct sunlight, scrape off excess soil and store them in vermiculite or peat moss in trays set where there is good air circulation. Be sure cannas and dahlias do not dry out too much, and sprinkle them lightly with water if they start to shrivel. Check on your bulbs every two to three weeks during the winter and discard rotted bulbs. The best temperature range for begonias, cannas and dahlias is 45° to 50°F; for gladiolas, 35° to 40°F.

Q: *How can I tell which side is up on my bulbs?*
A: The most heartbreaking question we have ever received about bulbs was, "I just planted several hundred tulip bulbs. The pointy side goes down, doesn't it?" Tulips, daffodils, hyacinths, and allium are planted with the pointy side up. Generally bulbs have a recognizably flat basal plate with old roots growing from it. This goes down. If there is a concave side and a convex side (begonias, gladiolas), the convex side goes down. The scales on lily bulbs point up. If new growth can be seen, as is sometimes the case with *Crocus, Colchicum* and *Canna*, this goes up. If you are completely at a loss (*Anemone blanda* and *Caladium* seem to offer no clues), plant the bulb sideways; the sprouts will eventually emerge. *Ranunculus* goes with the "fingers" down. Look for eyes on dahlias, at the end of the tuber; this end goes up.

Q: *How deep should bulbs be planted?*
A: The general rule is three

times as deep as the bulb is tall. Most daffodils, hyacinths and lilies should be planted 6 to 8 inches deep, and the same distance apart. Crocus and smaller bulbs should be planted 3 to 4 inches deep. Plant tulips deeper, 9 to 10 inches, to prolong their life span—this will help prevent them from splitting apart.

Q: What should I feed my bulbs and when?
A: Try Bulb Booster 9-9-6 in the fall to promote root growth. DO NOT fertilize after the bulb finishes flowering; the bulb is going dormant and doesn't need a large meal right before it goes to bed! Don't let fertilizer touch the bulb. When you plant, mix the fertilizer with the soil at the bottom of the hole and put a little more soil on top of this mix. When fertilizing previously planted bulbs, scratch the fertilizer into the soil in a ring around the bulb. Avoid high-nitrogen fertilizers, such as lawn fertilizers, because they encourage foliage growth at the expense of flowers.

GENERAL PROBLEMS

Q: My bulbs came up but didn't bloom.
A: It is possible that, (1) The foliage was removed too early last year and not enough energy was stored in the bulb over the winter. (2) The location is too shady, or the weather was too overcast. (3) They were stressed by fighting off insect or disease problems. (4) The fertilizer you are using is too high in nitrogen, so flower production is sacrificed for foliage growth. (5) The bulbs were recently forced, and they need one more year to recover. (6) They are too close together and compete for nutrients and moisture. (7) They were planted too late for good root growth in fall. (8) They were not chilled long enough, and your warm climate is not suitable for the bulbs you are growing. (9) The bulbs you planted are intended to bloom in another season.

Q: My bulbs performed well the first year after I planted them, but not this year, their second year. What happened?
A: The performance of this year's bulbs depends on the cultural environment last year. For their first year, the bulbs' performance depended on the ideal environment they experienced in Holland. The second year depends on your own garden conditions, which may be less than perfect. Review the requirements for each bulb—consider location, weather and insect and disease problems—and make any changes you feel would help. Dig some of the bulbs up to see if they suffer from rot, maggots or cutworms.

Q: My tulips were only 6 inches tall this year when they bloomed. They were 24 inches last year. Why?
A: This happens when unusually warm weather causes the bulbs to emerge early and then the weather turns cold again quickly. The cold prevents the stalk from growing taller. Sometimes the bulbs will bloom if the buds emerge when the weather is warm.

Q: My daffodils had flower buds that dried up. What happened?
A: This condition is called "bud blasting." It is caused by poor weather conditions, such as a very wet spring or cold temperatures, just when the buds are forming. It can also be caused by a disease such as botrytis. Some varieties, particularly old-fashioned daffodils, are especially prone to bud blasting.

Q: I got my bulbs too late to plant this fall. Can I plant them in the spring?
A: Bulbs should be planted by December if possible. You can consider forcing them, or try planting when the soil is workable. If you plant in early spring, they will grow, but they will bloom later or not at all. The best thing is to force them inside this year and plant them out in the garden next fall.

Q: My tulips fall apart when I bring them inside for cut flowers. How can I prevent this?
A: Cut your tulips before they open, early in the morning. Beat some egg white and, with a cotton swab or camel-hair brush, lightly "glue" the tips of the petals together. Don't use too much egg white or darker-colored tulips will look frosted.

Q: *My bulbs arrived mushy. Will they be all right?*
A: No; discard them and ask for your money back.

Q: *My bulbs are blooming at different times this year as compared to last year. Will this always happen?*
A: The first year they usually bloom a little later because they may have had abbreviated root growth in fall. After they are established they will bloom more regularly, although bloom times will always be affected by variable spring weather.

Q: *I planted my tulips in large containers on my patio. None came up! Why?*
A: Planting bulbs in containers outside is a little more complicated than planting them in the ground. It is important that the container have drainage holes or the bulbs will rot. The container will also freeze and thaw more quickly than the ground, especially if the container is in full sun. It may not be a good idea to plant bulbs in containers in Zones 3 and 4, and possibly 5. If you do, plant them in a movable container, one you can transfer to a sheltered location, out of the sun, but still colder than 45°F. Water occasionally if the container is in an unheated shed or garage. If you cannot move the container, cover it with several feet of leaves or pine boughs to protect it from the sun. Heap boughs or leaves around the sides to protect the container from temperature extremes.

DISEASE

Q: *My bulbs arrived with mold on them. Will they be all right?*
A: Bluish mold is penicillium mold, only a surface mold. This grows during shipment because of poor air circulation. If the bulbs are firm, you can wash the mold off and plant. White mold is a sign of fusarium, and can be accompanied by a sour smell, soft basal plate and oozing of liquid from the bulb. Wash off firm bulbs. If the bulbs are soft, smell bad, are hollow or have liquid oozing from them, discard them. If there is only a small amount of sooty mold and the bulb is firm, wash it off and plant the bulb. Discard if soft.

FORCING

Q: *My amaryllis* (Hippeastrum) *bulb isn't growing and I started it two months ago. What's wrong?*
A: Sometimes amaryllis can take a long time to emerge, sometimes they start the next day. Be patient with your bulb! Water it thoroughly at first, then sparingly until it begins to emerge. As long as the bulb is firm and there are slivers of green leaves visible at the top, the flowers and foliage will emerge.

Q: *Can I plant* Narcissus *daffodil bulbs outdoors after forcing? Will they bloom next year?*
A: Paperwhite narcissus are not hardy and should be discarded after they bloom; southern gardeners can try them in the garden. Hardy bulbs, such as 'Tête-à-Tête', can be planted outdoors after blooming or the following fall. Keep watering the bulbs after bloom and keep them in the sun. Allow the foliage to die naturally, as if they were outside. Then take them out of the soil, store them cool and dry until fall and plant in the garden with your other fall-planted bulbs. They will probably not bloom the first year, but should the following year. Bulbs cannot be forced twice.

Q: *My forced hyacinth bulbs produce miniature flowers close to the base of the plant. Why?*
A: Good root growth is as important for forced bulbs as it is for the bulbs in your garden, and poor flowering results from poor root growth. Hyacinths should be kept cool, about 50°F, after you start them for about two weeks. This encourages root growth. In a hyacinth glass, bring them gradually to room temperature when the roots are 4 inches long.

Q: *My forced hyacinths grow so tall they fall over. What's wrong?*
A: You brought them into warm temperatures too quickly and they grew too tall. Stakes can help hold them upright; 65°F is the best temperature for forcing bulbs indoors.

GENERAL INFORMATION

Q: I get a rash from handling my hyacinth bulbs!
A: Many people have an allergic reaction to hyacinth bulbs. This is not caused by a chemical treatment. Many people in the bulb industry wear gloves when handling hyacinth bulbs.

Q: My Caladium was planted six weeks ago, after the last frost, and it still hasn't come up. Will it?
A: *Caladium* can emerge any time from two to eight weeks after planting, depending on the soil temperature and moisture. One year it may come out by the end of May, the next not until the Fourth of July. Check to make sure the tubers are planted with the growth side up and that they are firm and healthy.

Q: I just received my colchicums and they are blooming in the bag! Will they be all right?
A: They'll be fine. We send colchicums out around the time they bloom, in late August or early September. You can enjoy the bloom before you plant the bulbs by placing the bulbs in a shallow bowl or plate without soil or water. Plant them after the flowers fade.

Q: What does DNI mean for daffodils?

A: *DNI* is used in describing the size of daffodils. DNI is the largest size and should have at least two "noses," DNII is smaller, with two noses, and DNIII is a single nose. Burpee tries to obtain the largest daffodil bulbs available for each variety, except in the case of bulbs for naturalizing. We offer smaller sizes for naturalizing bulbs because they are planted more easily and are more economical. Turn to page 8 to see the variety in bulb size.

Q: Why are species tulip bulbs so small?
A: Species tulips are the wildflowers of the tulip world, and like many wildflowers, their flowers, forms and bulbs are smaller than those of their cultivated descendants. They tend to last longer in the garden and are excellent to use as naturalizing plants.

Q: Which bulbs can be collected from the wild?
A: Much attention has been given recently to the problem of collected wild plants being sold commercially in the bulb industry. We are very pleased that consumers are becoming aware of this important issue and we are proud to present our policy of not selling or buying bulbs known or suspected to have been collected from the wild. We will purchase only bulbs that are nursery propagated, not just nursery grown. We don't sell *Trillium grandiflorum, Cypripedium acaule* (lady's-slipper orchid), *Erythronium* sp. (except 'Pagoda', which is propagated by approved methods) and *Sternbergia*, because they can't be successfully nursery propagated.

Beware when offered some species tulips (including *Tulipa praecox), Narcissus* sp. (especially miniatures in the *triandrus, cyclamineus, asturiensis* and *Pseudonarcissus* species), *Erythronium* (except 'Pagoda'), many *Fritillaria* sp., *Cypripedium* and *Pleione* orchids, *Cyclamen, Eranthis, Galanthus* and *Leucojum* sp. and many *Anemone blanda* varieties. Complete and up-to-date lists of endangered wild species are available through the National Resources Defense Council. Contact them at 1350 New York Avenue, NW, Washington, DC 20005.

Please also write or call for a free Burpee catalog:

W. Atlee Burpee & Company
300 Park Avenue
Warminster, PA 18974

215–674–9633

THE USDA PLANT HARDINESS MAP OF THE UNITED STATES

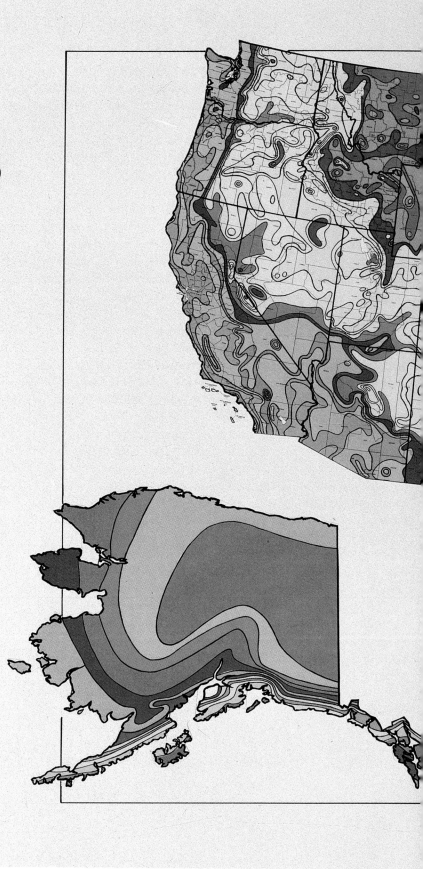

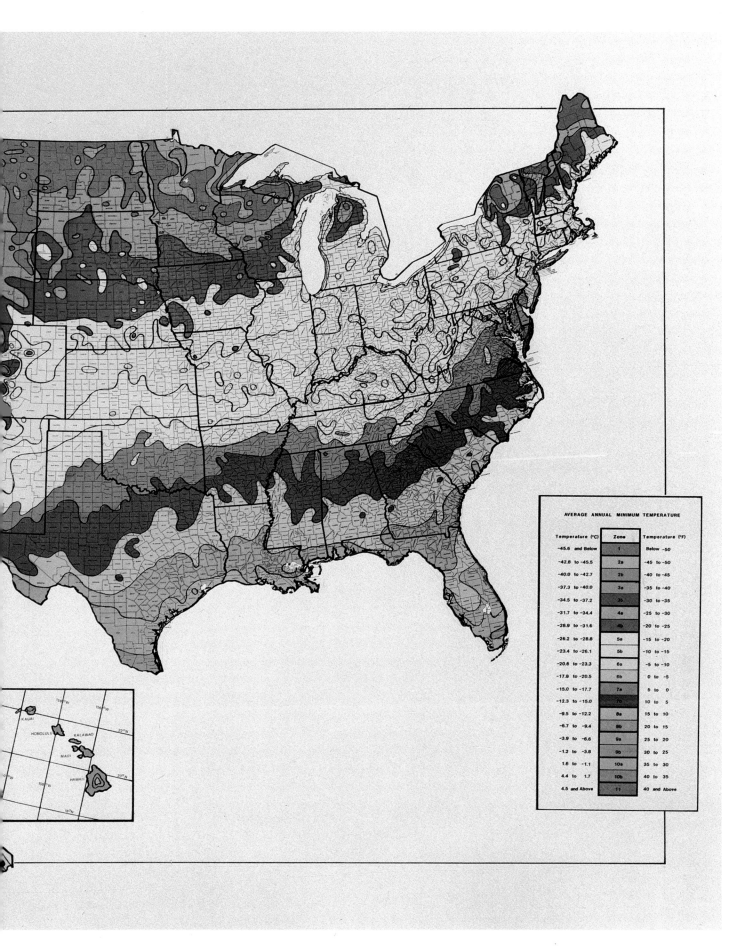

AVERAGE ANNUAL MINIMUM TEMPERATURE

Temperature (°C)	Zone	Temperature (°F)
-45.6 and Below	1	Below -50
-42.8 to -45.5	2a	-45 to -50
-40.0 to -42.7	2b	-40 to -45
-37.3 to -40.0	3a	-35 to -40
-34.5 to -37.2	3b	-30 to -35
-31.7 to -34.4	4a	-25 to -30
-28.9 to -31.6	4b	-20 to -25
-26.2 to -28.8	5a	-15 to -20
-23.4 to -26.1	5b	-10 to -15
-20.6 to -23.3	6a	-5 to -10
-17.8 to -20.5	6b	0 to -5
-15.0 to -17.7	7a	5 to 0
-12.3 to -15.0	7b	10 to 5
-9.5 to -12.2	8a	15 to 10
-6.7 to -9.4	8b	20 to 15
-3.9 to -6.6	9a	25 to 20
-1.2 to -3.8	9b	30 to 25
1.6 to -1.1	10a	35 to 30
4.4 to 1.7	10b	40 to 35
4.5 and Above	11	40 and Above

POPULAR HARDY BULBS—PLANTING CHART

NAME OF BULB	BLOOMING TIME (ZONE 6)*	HEIGHT	PREFERRED LIGHT CONDITIONS	PLANTING DEPTH	SPACING	REMARKS
Snowdrops (Galanthus)	Late February-early March	3–4″	Full sun or light shade	2–3″	2–4″	Plant in early fall. Needs moist soil. Leaves wither soon after flowers. Naturalize in grass and beneath deciduous trees. Can be forced. Zones 3–9.
Snow Crocus (Crocus)	Early March	3–4″	Full sun or part shade	3–4″	2–6″	Plant in large colonies; in warm, sheltered place for earliest bloom. Thrives in rock gardens or under low groundcovers. Increases rapidly. Forces well. Zones 3–8.
Winter Aconite (Eranthus hyemalis)	Early March	3–4″	Part shade	2–3″	3–4″	Soak tubers 24 hours in water before planting. Good in rock gardens or naturalized with snowdrops or snow crocus. Zones 4–9.
Spring Snowflake (Leucojum vernum)	Early March	6–9″	Full sun or part shade	3–4″	2–6″	Plant early in humusy soil, in colonies of 10 to 20 bulbs. Good in shady borders with ferns and wildflowers, or in rock garden. Zones 3–8.
Glory-of-the-Snow (Chionodoxa)	March	4–5″	Full sun or light shade	3–4″	1–3″	Plant in large colonies under deciduous trees; or naturalize. Flowers last 3–4 weeks. Beautiful with cyclamineus daffodils. Can be forced. Zones 3–10.
Daffodil (Cyclamineus)	March-April	6–12″	Full sun	6–8″	4–6″	Plant in warm, sheltered spot in rock garden or narrow border. Naturalizes well; increase rapidly. Zones 6–10.
Crocus	March-April	3–6″	Full sun or part shade	2–4″	2-6″	For earliest bloom, plant as early as possible in a sunny, protected spot. Best in groups of a single color. Naturalizes well; multiplies rapidly. Leaves mature somewhat slowly. Good in groundcovers. Force well. Zones 3–8.
Tulip (Species and Kaufmanniana)	March-April	4–12″	Full sun	3–16″	3–6″	Excellent in rock gardens and foreground plantings with squills and glory-of-the-snow. Zones 3–7 (and parts of Zones 8–10; check locally).
Puschkinia	March-April	4–6″	Full sun or part shade	2–3″	2–3″	Plant early. Very fragrant; naturalizes well. Good in rock gardens and foreground plantings, especially with evergreen shrubs or daffodils. Increases rapidly. Can be forced. Zones 3–10.
Daffodil (Giant trumpet, large-cupped, double-flowered and others)	April	8–24″	Full sun or part shade	7–8″	6–8″	Plant early in rich soil. Naturalize or plant in borders or under deciduous trees. Increases rapidly. Leaves mature rather slowly. Excellent for cutting or for forcing indoors. Lovely with 'Red Emperor' tulips. Zones 4–10.

*Average blooming time in Hardiness Zone 6. Blooming time in colder regions (Zones 4 and 5) may be later, in warmer regions (Zones 7 and 8) somewhat earlier. Annual and regional variations in weather conditions will also affect blooming time.

Name of Bulb	Blooming Time (Zone 6)*	Height	Preferred Light Conditions	Planting Depth	Spacing	Remarks
Siberian Squill *(Scilla siberica)*	April	6″	Full sun or part shade	2–3″	3–6″	Plant in large clumps under deciduous trees, in rock garden or in foreground of border. Pretty with daffodils. Foliage matures quickly. Zones 3–8.
Dogtooth Violet *(Erythronium)*	April	6–24″	Light shade	2–3″	2–3″	Needs moist soil rich in humus. Pretty at the base of trees. Zones 3–9.
Grape Hyacinth *(Muscari)*	April	6–10″	Full sun or light shade			For rock gardens or foreground of border with early double tulips, bleeding heart or daffodils. Good for cutting or forcing. Zones 2–10.
Tulips (Early-single, early-double and Fosteriana)	April	13–30″	Full sun	6–12″	6–8″	Good in the border in front of later tulips; lovely with white daffodils, candytuft, bleeding heart and grape hyacinths. Can be forced. Zones 3–7.
Hyacinth	April	10″	Full sun or part shade	4–5″	4–8″	Plant in groups of 5 or more of a color. Good in front of flowering shrubs, with daffodils and early tulips. Try blue hyacinths with yellow violas or pansies. Superb for forcing. Zones 5–10.
Crown Imperial *(Fritillaria imperialis)*	April	3–4″	Light shade or full sun	5–7″	8″	Likes sweet (alkaline), very well drained soil. Add lime if necessary. Good with white daffodils and Fosterana tulips. Zones 3–9.
Checkered Lily *(Fritillaria meleagris)*	April	6–12″	Light shade or full sun	3–4″	3–4″	Likes moist soil, rich in humus. Shows up well against a rock or tree trunk. Naturalize or plant in semishady border. Zones 3–9.
Tulips (Greigii hybrids, Mendel and Darwin hybrids)	April–May	8–30″	Full sun	6–12″	5–6″	May be planted until late fall, before ground freezes. Excellent for cutting. Weather-resistant blooms. Pretty with candytuft. Zones 3–7.
Tulips (Darwin, Rembrandt, Cottage and other May-flowering types)	May	15–30″	Full sun	6–12″	6–8″	Plant several varieties for a long span of color. Plant in drifts of one color, blending or contrasting with drifts of other colors. Find for rock gardens, perennial and shrub borders. Light-colored varieties striking against evergreens. Excellent for cutting. Zones 3–7.
Wood Hyacinth *(Endymion hispanicus)*	May	12–15″	Part shade or shade	4–5″	6″	Plant in groups in the shrub border or under deciduous trees. Increases very rapidly. Lovely with pink azaleas, Darwin tulips, primroses or in front of ferns. Zones 4–8.
Allium, Yellow *(A. Moly)*	May–June	10″	Light shade	3–4″	2–4″	Good in rock garden or foreground of border with forget-me-nots. Zones 4–10.
Allium, Giant *(A. giganteum)*	June–July	48–60″	Full sun	5–6″	12–18″	Flower umbels up to 6″ across. Plant at back of border. Wonderful for cutting and drying. Zones 6–10.

POPULAR HARDY BULBS—PLANTING CHART (cont.)

Name of Bulb	Blooming Time (Zone 6)*	Height	Preferred Light Conditions	Planting Depth	Spacing	Remarks
Hardy Amaryllis *(Lycoris)*	August	24–36"	Full sun or part shade	4–6"	6–10"	Leaves mature and fade before flower stalks appear. Most useful in semi-shady border or planted with ferns. Fragrant. Zones 5–10.
Hardy Cyclamen *(C. neapolitanum)*	September– October	4–5"	Light shade	½"	6–8"	Plant in rich soil where they can be easily seen. Thrive under deciduous trees. Plantings should not be disturbed. Zones 5–9.

INDEX

(NOTE: Italicized page numbers refer to captions.)

I am happy to express my deep gratitude to the many people who have helped me while I was writing this book. Many thanks go to my husband and partner, Carter F. Bales, Martha Kraska and Gina Norgard for providing me with unending help, support and love and to Alice R. Ireys, my close friend and mentor.

I am indebted to horticulturist Chela Kleiber who coordinated the question and answer section of this book; Eileen Kearney and Jonathan Burpee and the Burpee Customer Service department; to photography coordinator Barbara Wolverton and administrative assistant Elda Malgieri.

At Prentice Hall I would like to thank Anne Zeman, publisher, editor and gardener, whose watchful eye, patience, enthusiasm and belief in these books have made them a reality; Rebecca Atwater, whose twist of a phrase and a change of a word have greatly improved and polished these books; Rachel Simon for her patience and thoroughness.

Photography Credits

Agricultural Research Service USDA
Bales, Suzanne Frutig
Billhardt, Elizabeth
Cresson, Charles O.
Davids & Royston Bulb Co., Inc.
Fell, Derek
Harper, Pamela
Horticultural Photography, Corvallis, Oregon
International Bloembollen Centrum
Rokach, Allen
Schreiner's Iris Gardens
W. R. VANDERSCHOOT OF VA., INC.

Drawings by Michael Gale

Garden Designers:
Suzanne F. Bales (pages 6, 10, 18, 19, 22, 26, 29, 30, 38); Coleman (page 11); Ruth Levitan (page 15); Winterthur Gardens (page 17); Adele S. Mitchel (page 25)